THE
BOOK
OF
NATURE

THE ASTONISHING
BEAUTY OF GOD'S FIRST
SACRED TEXT

BARBARA MAHANY

BROADLEAF BOOKS
MINNEAPOLIS

THE BOOK OF NATURE
The Astonishing Beauty of God's First Sacred Text

30 29 28 27 26 25 24   1 2 3 4 5 6 7 8 9

The Library of Congress has cataloged the first edition as follows:

LCCN: 2023279271
LC Classification: BT695.5 .M343 2023

Cover image: leaf border - denisik11/GettyImages; birds- mrsopossum/GettyImages
Cover design: Olga Grlic

Hardcover ISBN: 978-1-5064-7351-2
eBook ISBN: 978-1-5064-7352-9
Paperback ISBN: 979-8-8898-3560-8

Note to Readers: The author recognizes that writers from another time often used male pronouns in reference to God; in those few instances where that occurs in these pages, the author has chosen to not change the original language, as spoken or written in centuries or decades past, and apologizes in advance if that language is off-putting to any reader. All references to God are gender-inclusive when written by the author. It is the author's deep hope that a spirit of inclusivity is present throughout.

Praise for *The Book of Nature:*
The Astonishing Beauty of God's First Sacred Text

"Mahany's lyrical, thoughtful, most recent work beautifully complements her shelf of awe-inspired books about nature and will appeal to fans of Shauna Niequist and Anne Lamott."

—*Booklist*

"For those in the Christian faith who grew up learning about God only from Bible lessons, *The Book of Nature* provides permission to wonder, get curious, and find God in the tiny details of a sprouting garden, a forest glade, birds in flight, or the moon. By showing readers how many respected theologians, seminarians, desert mothers and fathers, tribal leaders, and saints found God in nature, Mahany reminds us that there are different ways to encounter God all around us, beyond just in scripture."

—*BookPage*

"This is definitely a read-slowly kind of book. Happily for those of us who identify more as empirical than mystical, the former nurse writes that knowing scientific explanations for what she observes enhances rather than diminishes her awe."

—*Milwaukee Journal Sentinel*

"Mahany urges readers to be equally attentive so they will notice and fall in love with what she calls 'God's first sacred text' and what St. Augustine called 'the book of nature'—the natural world in which we live. She argues that our failure to be attentive is costing us a great deal, including experiences of the presence of the living God."

—*National Catholic Reporter*

"To read Mahany's meditations, and take in the 'Litany of Astonishment' that follows each of the sections, is to reengage with *The Book of Nature*. Perhaps we can stop and smell the roses or notice the patterns in the snow and rain. Perhaps we can take notice of God's presence as the creator and lover of creation. This doesn't mean we make nature an idol to worship, but rather, as we venerate this gift, caring for it (We are called to be its stewards, are we not?), we can give glory to God the creator."

—*Word&Way*

"Regardless of where one's spirituality (or lack of it) may lie, Barbara Mahany's *The Book of Nature* is a deeply rich celebration of the ageless overlap between religion and many faces of the natural world—the "Book of Nature" to which mystics, monks and others have turned for insight into the sacred. Best of all, this thought-provoking exploration is wrapped in Mahany's luscious and luminous writing, which makes every page a delight."

—**Scott Weidensaul**, author of *A World on the Wing*

"Attention is among the deepest forms of integrity. In *The Book of Nature*, Barbara Mahany pays attention. She doesn't look *through* nature, she looks *at* nature and there, sees the mysteries that make and unmake us. In an age of environmental threat and neglect, Barbara Mahany's book is a theological, poetic and devoted plea for attention to our most fundamental constitution: matter—and everything that comes from it, including us."

—**Pádraig Ó Tuama**, host of *Poetry Unbound* from On Being Studios

"*The Book of Nature* is an invitation to step into the newness of each day: sunrise, garden, forest, waters, nightfall. These pages reflect both awe and heartbreak, a pause when our world feels on fire, and the climate crisis calls us to collective lament, communion, and action."

—**Mallory McDuff**, author of *Love Your Mother: 50 States, 50 Stories, and 50 Women United for Climate Justice*

"Following in and deepening the footsteps of the Desert Mothers and Fathers, Barbara Mahany's *The Book of Nature* invites you to engage with nature as the body of God: to know that all life is the happening of a nondual Aliveness called by many names. Calling to a humanity drunk on transcendence and desperate to escape from Nature and our responsibility to Her, *The Book of Nature* reveals the sobering immanence of God as the Source and Substance of all reality."

—**Rabbi Rami Shapiro**, author of *Judaism Without Tribalism*

"Lovely and smart reflections—the perfect book to slip into a rucksack on a day you're planning a wander through the larger world!"

—**Bill McKibben**, author *The Flag, the Cross, and the Station Wagon*

THE BOOK
OF NATURE

To my boys, always to my boys:
Blair, and our very own homegrown double bylines,
Will and Teddy.
You are my everything, always, everywhere.

CONTENTS

THE HEAVENLY

Then the Lord answered Job out of the whirlwind:

"Where were you when I laid the foundation of the earth?
Tell me, if you have understanding.
Who determined its measurements—surely you know! . . .
Or who laid its cornerstone
when the morning stars sang together
and all the heavenly beings shouted for joy? . . .

"Have you commanded the morning since your days began,
and caused the dawn to know its place,
so that it might take hold of the skirts of the earth,
and the wicked be shaken out of it? . . .

"Has the rain a father,
or who has begotten the drops of dew?
From whose womb did the ice come forth,
and who has given birth to the hoarfrost of heaven? . . .

"Can you lift up your voice to the clouds,
so that a flood of waters may cover you?
Can you send forth lightnings, so that they may go
and say to you, 'Here we are'? . . .

"Is it by your wisdom that the hawk soars,
and spreads its wings toward the south?
Is it at your command that the eagle mounts up
and makes its nest on high?"

—Excerpts from Job 38 and 39, God's soliloquy

HOW I LEARNED TO READ
THE BOOK OF NATURE:
A FOREWORD

It began in the unlikeliest of ways. There I was, a half-hour deep into a radio talk show, impishly titled *How to Be a Holy Rascal*, with a rabbi whose poetry and prayers in our synagogue's prayer book had often made my knees go limp, with that frisson that comes when words, like a truth-seeking missile, pierce the heart. Poets have that way of putting to words the otherwise ineffable, the unnoticed that's long been right before your eyes.

We, the rabbi and I, were talking about my very first book, *Slowing Time: Seeing the Sacred outside Your Kitchen Door*, a collection of prayerful essays and a hodgepodge of wonderments that unfurls season by season, very much rooted not only in the ramshackle runaway garden outside my kitchen door, but in the whole of creation stuffed in my quarter-acre plot here in a leafy little burg along Lake Michigan's shoreline. The good rabbi was peppering me with probing questions, listening along, when all of a sudden he piped in: "*Slowing Time* reads like midrash to the Book of Nature." He had me at midrash, ancient rabbinic commentary, the practice of bringing sacred imagination to a scriptural text. It's not every day that a lifelong Irish Catholic has terms like *midrash* tossed her way and certainly not in a way that pins her to the practice.

But if midrash got my attention, it was *Book of Nature* that stopped me. Was there an actual thing, a book filled with pages of nature's wonderments? And if so, why would anyone—be they rabbi or scholar or priest—be offering up commentary? How had I missed it, this book that I sensed was not your everyday field guide but something so awe-infused it comes with capital letters?

I set out to find out, beginning where many a quest for knowledge begins these days: Googling. Indeed, there exists such a so-titled tome, though it's metaphorical in name, and its roots are as Christian as anything. It's ancient. It goes back, long before it was named, to preliterate civilizations, to eras and epochs and dynasties and tribes before pages were printed, long before script. It goes back to the first human stirrings on the planet, when the first someone looked to the sky and felt some epiphany. Or suffered the blows of a harvest gone *pfft* when some almighty scourge drowned or devoured or way overbaked it. Ancient peoples read the Book of Nature as the first sacred text, the text of all of creation, inscribed and unfurled by a God present always and everywhere.

Turns out, the ancients weren't the last ones to read it, though it wasn't so titled till millennia later. Importantly, the twelfth century is when the ordering of science and the systemization of the natural world seeped into Christian thought, an enlightenment that crystallized an earlier ecclesiastical sense that through nature—clearly God's handiwork—humankind might glean the workings of the One who'd sculpted the mountains and parted the seas, and come to a deeper knowledge therein. Put simply: God had infused the natural world with symbol and meaning, and if only we read what's there in the trees and the storms and the stars and the hives, we might more fully comprehend the Creator. Not unlike pondering a parable, unpuzzling a proverb.

That emergent thinking, accelerating into the early Renaissance, when science was making sense of the seen and the unseen, brought with it a tension, and for some the start of a schism, when scientific inquiry is said to have brought a table of contents—its subjects readily indexed—to the idea that nature itself was a source for divine revelation. Literal explication threatened to shove aside allegorical interpretation.

But for others—and I count myself among them—the science itself eluci-dated all the more brilliantly the text whose meaning as a whole could now be discerned and through which we might encounter its author. (The first tome actually titled *Book of Nature* is thought to be one dated 1481; a bit more than a century later, in 1615, none other than Galileo, in a letter to the grand duchess of Tuscany, wrote that "God is known first through Nature, and then again, more particularly, by doctrine," quoting Tertullian, a second-century Chris-tian theologian, and hinting at an imperative to pair the two sacred texts, nature and Scripture.)

Through the ages, tracing through centers of knowledge and wisdom East and West, and across every continent, right up to the now, the Book of Nature has been the one sacred text that needs no translation; it's unfurled without words, composed in an alphabet of seashell and moonbeam, the flight of the birds, and even the plundering of nests. Its readers are prophets and poets, mystics and monastics, Christians and Jews, Buddhists and Muslims, Lakota and Anishinaabe, and those who'd not set a foot in any houses of worship.

I came to the Book of Nature Jewishly—and not just because a rabbi was the first to utter the words in my presence. No, I married a Jew. And, as a life-long, devout, liberal Catholic who was hooking my life to that of an observant Jew, I dove right in, to every myriad and facet of this religion that had long fascinated me. We'd decided, my beloved and I, that we were going to try to make it work, two religions under one roof. All along, I kept going to church (lately, an Anglo-Catholic one). My beloved joined me there, and I joined him in synagogue. We vowed we would raise our children to be fluent in both. Two religions—sometimes exuberantly, often quietly, always inquisitively—side by side, under one roof.

Soon after we married, I discovered Shabbat, the sacred pause at the end of the workweek, God's holy command to put down our toil and enter sanc-tified time. Dutifully, and lovingly, each Friday night, I pulled out the pair of Sabbath candlesticks and the kiddush cup, and covered the challah; I memo-rized the Hebrew blessings, the ones we recited over kindled light, the bread of the earth, and the fruit of the vine. (In time, too, I learned the blessings to be said over children, in our case two boys, born eight years apart.)

Then came the prayers: so many punctuated with celestial reference—morning star and new moon—or the earthly—the flocks and the fields, the birds of the air, the lily among the thorns. Even the mitzvot, or commands, bow to creation. At the harvest festival of Sukkot, you're to leave open the roof of your sukkah (or makeshift shelter) so you can count the stars in the heavens. On Shabbat, you're to light the Sabbath candles eighteen minutes before the western horizon swallows the sun. And, according to Jewish law, Shabbat doesn't draw to a close until three medium-sized stars (*tzeit ha-kokhavim*) appear in the inky twilight of Saturday's dusk.

And so, when I came to the Book of Nature, I was stirred not only by my Catholicism's sense of a deeply intimate God but also by Judaism's finer-grained reading of the cosmos. I found myself immersed in a newly palpable presence, a trace of the sacred etched in all creation. I was bumping up against a text of wonder and awe, authored by the God I'd always known, but never so perceptibly, in every turning of this holy earth.

Once I moved beyond Google, once I pulled from my bookshelves a handful of monks (Thomas Merton and David Steindl-Rast), poets (Mary Oliver, Rita Dove, David Whyte, and W. S. Merwin, among the many), Transcendentalists (the Concord duo, Henry David Thoreau and Ralph Waldo Emerson), and the great twentieth-century literary prophet (Annie Dillard), I moved back in time plucking the tomes of Hildegard of Bingen and Julian of Norwich, the ancient Celts, the T'ang Dynasty poet Li Po, and the Japanese master of haiku, Matsuo Bashō. I skipped around continents, from John Muir's and Henry Beston's America to Pablo Neruda's and Octavio Paz's Latin America, from Roger Deakin's and Robert Macfarlane's Great Britain, to Rumi's and Hafez's Persia, and the Desert Fathers and Mothers of Egypt. I read the believers (Francis of Assisi) and the maybe-nots (Loren Eiseley).

All these good souls and deep thinkers somehow illuminated every page and paragraph of the Book of Nature, every season and storm, every dollop of birdsong. Their work, to me, is like so many glorious medieval manuscripts, the holy labor of monks who spent their lives bent over sheets of vellum in the scriptorium, tracing biblical text with quill of peacock, crow, or eagle, and ink from insects, plants, burned bones, or bits of gold—each page a devotion enrobed in ornament.

Other times, I think reading the Book of Nature is like reading a page of Talmud, with the Mishnah and Gemara of stars and skies surrounded by the commentary of Hildegard and Hafez.

I read with my heart and my soul wide open. I read with my loam-stained mitts sunk deep in the earth, and my mud-splashed boots crunching the autumn woods. I read with my nose to the glass from my upstairs nook. I read while taking out the trash and when dumping sunflower seed in the backyard feeder. I read when the rain taps at my window and awakes me from slumber. I read when I open my eyes to an ice-crystal dawn.

And the more I read, the more I see and feel and hear. With my own eyes and flesh and ears—and soul. And the more I see what has always been: my God reaching out to me in all God's astonishments and beauties and wonders.

It's a book without end, and I'll never stop reading.

Every leaf of the tree
becomes a page of the sacred scripture
once the soul has learned to read.

—Sa'di Shirazi, thirteenth-century Persian poet

It was the Book of Nature,
written by the finger of God, which I studied . . .

—Paracelsus, sixteenth-century physician and philosopher

The texture of the world, its filigree and scrollwork, means that there is the
possibility for beauty here, a beauty inexhaustible in its complexity, which
opens to my knock, which answers in me a call I do not remember calling, and
which trains me to the wild and extravagant nature of the spirit I seek. . . .
The whole creation is one lunatic fringe.

—Annie Dillard, Pulitzer Prize–winning American author

READING THE
BOOK OF NATURE

*The book of nature is a fine and large piece of tapestry rolled up, which we
are not able to see all at once, but must be content to wait for the discovery
of its beauty, and symmetry, little by little, as it gradually comes to be more
and more unfolded.*

—Robert Boyle, seventeenth-century
natural philosopher and chemist

One of the first bibliographers to put a name to the Book of Nature
was Antony the Great, a third-century Egyptian Desert Father,
who when asked by a curious visitor how he managed to be so
learned with nary a book on a shelf, replied, "My book is the nature of created things, and as often as I have a mind to read the words of God, it is at
my hand." Theophan the Recluse, the nineteenth-century Russian Orthodox
saint, declared creation a "holy book filled with uncountable and wonderfully
different paragraphs." In the same century but a different landscape, Henry
David Thoreau is said to have walked his *sanctum sanctorum*, a grove of ancient
oaks or a stand of Eastern white pines, alert to the mystical, "more as sup-
plicant than naturalist." In his journal on September 7, 1851, he wrote, "If by
watching all day and all night, I may detect some trace of the ineffable, then
will it not be worth the while to watch?"

His life's work, as he saw it, was "to be always on the alert to find God in nature, to know his lurking-places, to attend all the oratorios, the operas, in nature."

I, too, am on lookout.

Mine is a quotidian geography. The undulations of my topography are of the humdrum variety. No sharp-chiseled summits, no crags in the rock. I live in the heartland, after all, a landscape long ago steamrolled into equanimity by Ice Age glaciers that erased most every speck of drama as they receded. Nowadays, the nearest flowing current to my old shingled house is a canal carved out of the prairie, one charged with curbing the flow of dreck into the lake, the great Lake Michigan, the one neighborhood landmark worthy of capital letters, the one whose roar I can pick out if I train my ears keenly amid the howlings of incoming wind or winter storm. The woods I call my own are habitat to the homeliest of flocks, ones most often cloaked in iterations of drab: chickadee, nuthatch, sparrow, siskin. We startle to any dab of color: blue jay, red-headed flicker, the perennial cardinal. Word travels fast if the barn owls swoop in; sightings spread with ferocity. We are a people of dialed-down expectation.

And yet I am attuned and on high alert to the filigree and bedazzlement of the author of it all, the one who paints the dawn in tourmaline streaks and salts the night sky in chalky, sometimes brilliant, flecks, the one who thought to quench the thirst of the migrating butterfly with mists of fog and remembered that baby birds might do well to memorize the star-stitched tracings far, far above the nursery that is the nest.

Mine is the God of sunrise and nightfall, the breath behind birdsong and breeze in the oaks. Mine is the God of a thousand voices, a thousand lights, and gazillions of colors. Whether I notice or not, mine is the God who never hits pause when it comes to creation: inventing, reinventing, tweaking, editing, starting from scratch all over again, day after day after heavenly day.

"By means of all created things, without exception, the divine assails us, penetrates us and moulds us," wrote Pierre Teilhard de Chardin, the French Jesuit paleontologist and philosopher, in the opening passages of *The Divine Milieu*, his 1957 text "for the waverers," those caught at faith's threshold, not in or not out. His words, apt for the Atomic Age, are apt for this moment, the Digital Age, as well. We imagine creation as "distant and inaccessible," Teilhard argued back then, as the threat of nuclear ash still hung in the air, "whereas in fact we live steeped in its burning layers. . . . The world, this palpable world, which we were wont to treat with the boredom and disrespect with which we habitually regard places with no sacred association for us, is in truth a holy place, and we did not know it."

His words are as true today as in the mid-twentieth century, when Hiroshima and the Holocaust shrouded the planet in apocalyptic vision, draped the beautiful and the blessed under light-blocking cloth. Ours now is a world lit up in digital glare. We stare into our phones instead of the stars, glued to our screens instead of the world in all its real-time rumblings and respirations. It's an ecology of loss; we're too often blind to creation. And the losses I worry about aren't only the ones tabulated by climatologists, counted in species decline and extinctions, waters rising and ice caps melting. The losses I tally are just as profound yet outside the bounds of the measurable: beauty, wonder, the wild, intimacy; knowing the world by the whorl of your fingertips, by the dew of the dawn under your toes. Most of all, there's a slipping away of a palpable sense of the sacred.

It needn't be. It shouldn't be.

Know it or not, seen or unseen, we dwell in the thick of the "grand volume of God's utterance," as the Celts—a people ever keen to the whisperings amid the sanctuary of earth and sea and sky—have long referred to it. Theirs is a posture that cuts across denominations, that speaks to all those who bow to the *mysterium tremendum*, that very awe before the universe, before which humanity both trembles and is fascinated.

As Loren Eiseley, the archeologist, anthropologist, and naturalist, once wrote, "Ever since man first painted animals in the dark of caves he has been responding to the holy, to the numinous, to the mystery of being and becoming, to what Goethe very aptly called 'the weird portentous.' Something inexpressible was felt to lie behind nature."

And that doesn't mean we need trek to the exotic to trip over the numinous. Holiness is just as likely lurking in the quotidian, in whatever patch of

9

tall grass or weeds you call your own. And, besides, the star-knotted night cloth is draped over all of our heads; so, too, the moon, the light that shines nightly in ever-shifting fractions, never the same twice in a row.

It's telling that two of the most profound in the annals of watchkeeping, Annie Dillard, the great pilgrim of Tinker Creek, and Thoreau, the woodsman of Walden Pond, never ventured too far from home. In her 1974 chronicle on solitude, Dillard's laser-eyed wanderings in the woods made a suburban watershed sound like a hallucinogenic wonderland, in much the same way Thoreau made Walden, a hardly-off-the-grid water hole a mere twenty-minute walk from his mother's house, the birthplace of timeless epiphanies. It's all in how you see.

Here's how Dillard saw it from her perch—a fallen sycamore trunk—on the banks of her Roanoke Valley creek, whether spying a giant water bug suck up a frog or watching a praying mantis lay eggs: "If the landscape reveals one certainty, it is that the extravagant gesture is the very stuff of creation. After one extravagant gesture of creation in the first place, the universe has continued to deal exclusively in extravagances, flinging intricacies and colossi down aeons of emptiness, heaping profusions on profligacies with ever-fresh vigor. The whole show has been on fire from the word go. . . . That which isn't flint is tinder, and the whole world sparks and flames."

It is an extravagance—indeed, a fiery one—pressed into the pages of the Book of Nature, the ancient theology that insists God's first revelation was spelled out in the alphabet letters of every leaf on every tree, in the sound and silence of every trill of birdsong, from the tiniest of caterpillars to the dome of heaven arced across the star-threaded sky.

While it's been argued that the wonders of creation cannot be adequately expressed in ink on paper—"Letters cannot contain it, letters cannot comprehend it," maintained a ninth-century Welsh poem—Thomas Aquinas, four centuries later, astutely seized the metaphor: "Sacred writings are bound in two volumes—that of creation and that of Holy Scripture."

It is thus that the paired-volume thinking came to be known, throughout the centuries, as the Two-Book theology, which holds that the presence of God is best apprehended through the tandem reading of creation—God's original sacred text—alongside Holy Scripture. As far back as the ninth century, in the early age of Celtic Christianity, John Scotus Eriugena, the greatest philosophical thinker to emerge from that distant edge of the habitable world, wrote in his *Homily on the Prologue to the Gospel of St. John* that the two books must be read together. According to Celtic scholar J. Philip Newell, Eriugena taught that "Christ moves among us in two shoes, as it were, one shoe being that of creation, the other that of the scriptures," and stressed the need to be alert and attentive to both.

The Two-Book metaphor permeated Western Christianity, to varying degrees at various times. But even more so, the central idea of a sacred cosmos had long been rooted in the East, infusing the teachings of Egyptian desert elders, Taoist philosophers, Buddhist Zen masters and lamas, Hindu sadhus, Muslim Sufi poets, and Jewish Hasids. Indigenous peoples the world over—Maasai in the grasslands of Kenya, Bedouin in the Syrian desert, Tamil in the Sri Lanka highlands, to name but a few—and certainly the First Nations dwellers on our own Turtle Island never abandoned the knowing that the terrestrial call—the whistling of wind, the eagle's cry, the burbling brook, the thrashing rapids—was, in each and every syntax, the voice of God.

The embeddedness of the divine in all creation is emphatically not to be confused with pantheism's point that God equals nature, the sense that God *is* the wind and water, sunlight and cloud. Rather, the lens through which I'm seeing is pan*en*theism, God *in* wind and water, not God *as* wind or water. Put another way: get rid of nature to the pantheist, and you get rid of God. Get rid of nature to the panentheist, and you see God all the more clearly. It's the stirrings and rumblings in nature that reveal the trace of the divine, that point toward the inexpressible, the immeasurable. We stare into the stars to glimpse the unfathomable.

"All the way back to the creation of the universe and the small quickenings of earth," writes Chickasaw Nation poet and novelist Linda Hogan, the Native people have understood "a form of sacred reason, different from ordinary reason, that is linked to forces of nature." The more those tribal elders seek to learn the world, "the closer they come to the spiritual," she explains. "There is a still place, a gap between worlds, spoken by the tribal knowings of thousands of years . . . [and] when we are silent enough, still enough, we take a step into such mystery, the place of spirit."

It's from this in-between borderland, according to this earliest wisdom, that something like a sacred bellows—mysterious and beyond earthly reason—inspires all of creation. It is the animating force of the wind, birthed where lightning and thunder, rain clouds and sun, begin without end. It is the cosmic quickening thought to spark the germination of the corn, and the breath behind the timber wolves' old song, the howl that breaks the northern night and stirs a timeless, nameless memory. It is not the realm of physics, nor botany, nor any earthly science; it is—to all who put their heart against the thrum of Gaia—from a realm beyond celestial.

It is the visible invisible, the tracing of the divine, etched across the cosmos.

This understanding of what John Keats called "the poetry of earth" inscribed in a holy book traces its roots to ancient Israel and the biblical poets and prophets, agrarian peoples straining to eke sustenance from the desert and the delta, who saw all of the natural world—from rainfall to mustard seed—as "where the truth of God is hidden."

For peoples steeped in the trials of survival, wholly dependent on heaven and earth, it's not hard to imagine that they sought—and found—in the wheeling rhythms of natural phenomena and the hardscrabble early-world labors of farming and herding and fishing, the analogies that pointed to wisdom. In time, this earthborn common sense—how to live wisely before God, as informed by seemingly immutable laws of nature—was inscribed in the books of Wisdom, or Wisdom literature, of the Hebrew Bible. Spilling with proverbs such as "whoever tends a fig tree will eat its fruit," or "go to the ant, you lazybones; consider its ways, and be wise," it reads, even now, like something of a farmer's almanac of a biblical kind.

Creation-centered spirituality flourished especially in the Celtic tradition, which reached deep into the mysticism of John the Evangelist, he who at the Last Supper leaned against the chest of Jesus and heard the heartbeat of God. The Celts embraced that hallowed image to inspire the practice of listening for the heartbeat of God in all of creation. Scottish mystic Alexander John Scott, among the nineteenth-century revivalists of Celtic spirituality, once wrote that creation "is a transparency through which a light of God is seen," and taught that "everywhere can be found the ladder that connects heaven and earth."

Those teachings nearly got waylaid not long after their dawning, and their principal disciple all but muzzled in dueling theologies and a power play of the early Christian church. It's a tale of just-missed extinction that goes like this: The fourth-century monk Pelagius, a prolific author and early apostle of Celtic tradition, had made his way in the early 380s from somewhere in Wales to distant Rome (despite being criticized by Saint Jerome for "walking at the pace of a turtle"). There, he gathered quite a following and dared to take on Augustine of Hippo, a driving force in Roman church circles who accused Pelagius of a host of failings, especially rejecting original sin. In fact, the slow-moving Celtic monk preached the blessedness of creation and taught, among other things, that "narrow shafts of divine light pierce the veil that separates heaven from earth." In his ageless letters, Pelagius beseeches us to open our innermost senses to the knowing of God, be it through Scripture or sacrament or the whole of creation, "to see with the eyes of the heart." It's a knowledge that comes from "some deeper part of the human being," writes Newell, "the way an infant comes to know its mother."

But Pelagius and his insights were unapologetically pushed to the corners of the Celtic world: the teacherly monk shunned as a heretic, banned from the Roman Empire, and excommunicated in the mid-summer of 418, after a bitter theological attack by Augustine. Banished to the hinterlands, the Celtic mission of the writerly monk didn't die, but rather was left alone. Pelagius's excommunication had the fortune or misfortune of coming around the time the Roman occupying army was ordered back to the continent, to stanch the flow of barbarian invasions, in the wake of the sacking of Rome. For two centuries, the Celts in their faraway monasteries honed their creation-inspired, God-in-all-things spirituality and kept it alive. The Roman way, though, embedded in church authority, widening the chasm between the mystery of creation and the mystery of God, cast the dominant shadow and hardened its influence. It all came to a head in 664, at the Synod of Whitby, in Northumbria, in the northeast of England, an assembly convened to settle once and for all the debate between the disparate theologies. The Roman mission of Augustine won out and effectively quashed Pelagius's Celtic mission. The tragedy of Whitby is that there wasn't room for *both* ways, and the Celtic way slowly faded. "More and more," Newell writes, "the 'holy place' was identified with the sanctuary of the church rather than the sanctuary of earth, sea and sky."

Ecclesial politicking wasn't the sole force pushing the Book of Nature and its author increasingly out of reach. Somewhere along the line, there seeped in the thinking that harnessing the wild equaled progress. The fiercer and faster we've barreled through the ages—Industrial, Machine, Atomic, Digital—the farther we've grown from the God of the unharnessed wild. If we can't sense that perceptible presence, if we don't think to walk in the woods in search of the holy, if we don't look into the heavens for something deeper than the stars, if the unbridled joy of a fledgling's first flight doesn't strike us as unscripted sacred instruction, then we're all but skipping over the first best text God ever gave us.

Which is why I'm so emphatically trying to read it.

One of the surest threads binding together the pages of this First Book, a sentient volume, is the old idea of the Deus absconditus, the hidden God, which means we live in the very presence of that God even in our hours of oblivion. It's an idea that draws from an ancient hadith, or saying, of the Prophet Muhammad, "I was a hidden treasure and I desired to be known." What's most stirring in that blessed claim is its palpable note of yearning, in this case *God's* yearning, God's yearning for *us*. We are the ones God awaits, the ones God hopes to quietly tap on the heart, to rouse, maybe even to startle to astonishment. There's a sadness, too, in that longing. And if you've an ounce of empathy—the capacity for slipping inside another's silhouette—you might feel the walls of your own chambered heart expanding, reaching toward the God who yearns for us, who since the dawn of, well, creation has dwelled to delight us with majesties and wonders and awe, writ prodigiously or in finest-grain intricacy.

The elusiveness, the catch-if-you-can of it is what takes my breath away. This is not a God inclined to clang me on the head, but rather to lie in wait, crouching low within the mystery, furled as the tight-fisted spiral of the fiddle-head fern, or the coiled depths of the chambered nautilus. "Wind and water, sunlight and cloud, dream and vision, bird and animal, thought and silence ebb and flow like so many veils before the Face of God," is how scholar and translator Christopher Bamford captures it in *The Voice of the Eagle*, his meditation on Eriugena's ninth-century Celtic Christian theology. As Bamford so aptly, poetically, puts it: "Mountains, grasses, and trees become his Gospels, clouds and animals his prophets."

Indeed, these are the gospels and the prophets to which I turn. Whose stirrings stir me. Whose lessons I imbibe.

I read intently the Book of Nature, even here in my humble plot of earth, one where the gnarled fingers of a towering locust tree reach into the night sky, all but pluck the stitches of star and sliver of moon from the vast velvet dome. Where a rambunctious tucked-away garden offers me respite, and a place for genuflection, amid the runaway brambles that aim to catch me by the ankles, should I dare to tiptoe past the tangles along the stepping-stone path.

Into its pages I step in the murky hour just before the dawn, before the rising sun stages its rehearsal, bleeds pink into the edge of night. It's where you might find me, nose pressed to the glass, when the softening winter sky at last exhales and the first tumble of snowflakes fall, blanketing the world in a quiet like no other. Or, at twilight, the in-between hour when day dissolves into darkness, when on a summer's eve I surrender to the rising surround sound of crickets and keep watch till the starkeepers trot out the stars.

In listening closely, and reading across the ages, I've noticed a collective, often feminine, attunement to the lifting of the veil; its poetries fine-focus my attentions, its leitmotif suggests quiet, close inspection: "God's soul is the wind rustling plants and leaves, the dew dancing on the grass, the rainy breezes making everything grow," wrote Hildegard of Bingen, the Benedictine abbess, mystic, and herbalist of the twelfth century. "All has been consecrated," wrote Catherine of Siena. Evelyn Underhill, the Anglo-Catholic mystic and pacifist, captured it breathtakingly when she recounted the words of Saint John of the Cross, who wrote that "God passes through the thicket of the world, and wherever his glance falls he turns all things to beauty."

And so the beautiful, the majestic, the intimate, and the sweeping is pressed onto the pages of the *librum naturae*, the Book of Nature. I read it all, every alphabet letter. Nearly every time, it catches me upside the heart.

I've likened it to being featherstroked on the chest, or up near my temples where thoughts wriggle like breeze through the bluestem. I've felt my knees wobble under the weight of it, the wonder of it. It prompts me, often, to crane my neck, a walking, gawking stargazer. It might catch me mid-musing, hauling the recycling out to the alley. If given my druthers, I'm inclined to keep watch by tucking myself into the folds of the earth, tend to prefer crouching down low, hiding myself amid the knives' blades of grasses that rise from the mounds along the sandy shore of Lake Michigan, minutes away from my house. Or under the cottonwoods, sacred to me—and to the Lakota, who hear a perpetual prayer as the leaves quake in the wind. My most prayerful pose is whenever I feel how trifling I am against the vast infinity of Elohim, the Creator. It evokes in me a reaching out toward God, an almost climbing into God's arms.

The remarkable thing is that this holiness is nearly impossible to escape. It's at once ubiquitous and ephemeral. Down here below the stars it comes in subtleties that might be overlooked, though sometimes—when the crack of thunder shakes you from your slumber—it's undeniable: the divine wields a weighty hammer.

Yes, God plays in all scales. In sweeping arcs of broad brushstroke: the cavernous dome of heaven in all its illimitable beauty. Or intimate and intricate, and take-your-breath-away: Have you ever watched a hummingbird's heart pulse against the bejeweled feathering of its Lilliputian chest?

We'd best pay attention, exquisite attention, if epiphany is where we aim to point our compass. The Japanese poet Bashō reminds us to be on the lookout for a "glimpse of the underglimmer." Dillard, again writing from Tinker Creek, cautioned that for all this profusion of holy exuberance, "we can only feel blindly of its hem."

So we go on our spelunking way, mindful, ever mindful of Ralph Waldo Emerson's blessed instructive that "the invariable mark of wisdom is to see the miraculous in the common." A humble path we trod a hundred times a week, a plot you might mistake for jumble of weeds, the most familiar nook or cranny just beyond our kitchen door, that might be the crosshair where "earth and heaven touch, interpenetrate, illuminate one another," in the words of Esther de Waal, one of the foremost Celtic scholars. You know it when you feel a quickening or a shivering in "that part of myself that is older than I am," as the incomparable Celts would put it.

And that—the barely perceptible but utterly certain presence—might be the one holy thing that we seek, an ancient and abiding echo, the bottomless well of the sacred that rests in each of our souls, yearning to be awakened, enlivened, rustled from sleep.

Indubitably: the song of creation will hum.

Or as the California poet and sage Robinson Jeffers once wrote, the natural music of God might be heard in "the old voice of the ocean, the bird-chatter of little rivers." And the excesses of God, Jeffers wrote in another poem, will be just as abundantly obvious from a Creator who thinks "to fling rainbows over the rain, and beauty above the moon," who tucks "secret rainbows on the domes of deep sea-shells," and who sees to it that "not even the weeds . . . multiply without blossom, nor the birds without music."

What if, in our short stint here on earth, in the flash-bang that is our lifetime, we miss the divine exuberance, God all but cupping our chins in God's palms and turning us toward the latest, greatest blessed thing? And what then are we to do with a world pummeled by so much inattention, the Blue Marble ravaged by the deadliest of sins: avarice and greed, rape and pillage, pride, lust, envy, gluttony, wrath, and, oh yes, sloth?

The lament is not new. The Book of Nature, for many, has been cobwebbed on a shelf, the holy wisdom of creation, the ongoing ever-ness of every day a new creation, cut off from sensibility. Oh, sure, the sun rose with raging fire and shone the whole day long. Birds chattered. And the meadow erupted in its muted tapestry. And at night, the stars never failed to flicker.

But we've lost the capacity to read the scripts in meadow and sky. It's one thing to glimpse a pretty sunset; it's a whole other thing to see the sunset and be drawn into the unshakable sense that there is a majesty and a divinity beyond our wildest comprehensions, and as surely as there is a God who paints the sky, peels open the apple blossom, and puts flight to the wing of the bird, there is a God who hears our deepest cries and the prayers we can barely put to whisper. The Book of Nature is the text that joins the two.

Herewith, a return to reading that Book.

The very meaning of Creation is seen to be an act of worship, a devoted proclamation of the splendour, the wonder, and the beauty of God. In this great Sanctus, all things justify their being and have their place. . . . "Wherein does your prayer consist?" said St. John of the Cross to one of his penitents. She replied: "In considering the Beauty of God, and in rejoicing that He has such beauty."

—Evelyn Underhill, twentieth-century English
theologian, mystic, and pacifist

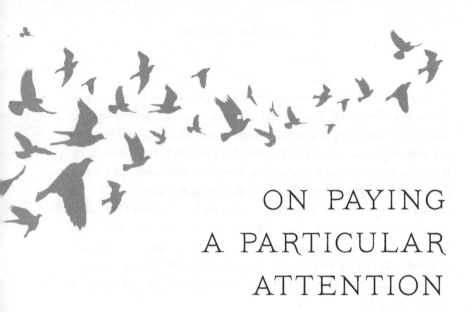

ON PAYING
A PARTICULAR
ATTENTION

Attention, taken to its highest degree, is the same thing as prayer.

—Simone Weil, twentieth-century French
philosopher, mystic, and political activist

The road to epiphany is attention.

As it ever has been. Across the millennia, the ones seeking the sacred—poets and prophets, mystics and everyday saints, holy vagabonds and run-of-the-mill antisomnambulists—stalk the earth attuned to susurrations and silence and the palpable sense of something deeply astir: the animating author of all the cosmos. It's a watchkeeping ever on watch. Peel back the wisdoms of East or West, plumb the canons of any civilization, listen to the thrum of Indigenous truth telling, and there you will find the spiritual practice of paying closest attention. On alert to the visible invisibility.

Mark Strand, the Pulitzer-winning poet laureate, boiled it down in plainspoken logical terms: "We're only here for a short while. And I think it's such a lucky accident, having been born, that we're almost obliged to pay attention."

Indeed, if, in this too-swift sprint that is our lives—"a faint tracing on the surface of mystery," in one poet's inscription—we are here to inch our way toward absorbing and being absorbed into the divine, thinning the veil between heaven and earth, then the surest way there is to crank up the senses, and not fall asleep on the clock. I've sometimes wondered if maybe our sensory components—those inner workings of the human species, the neurotransmitters by which we take notice—might have been God's after-thoughts (something of an editorial tweak, a rococo embellishment at the hour of creation) upon delighting in the whimsy of rainbows confettied across the sky and giggling aloud at, say, the great heron's curious footprint, an appendicular trace once described as "an ideogram at the end of the cal-ligrapher's brush."

God, it so happens, is not of miserly constitution.

All through the ages, there's been an unbroken tradition of spiritual-ists pointing the way, all but tracing a finger across the pages of the Book of Nature. We needn't look to the fringe. The Belgic Confession of 1561, a cornerstone of Reformed doctrine, one of the earliest such statements of faith, spelled it out in article 2, titled "The Means by Which We Know God": "That universe is before our eyes like a beautiful book in which all creatures, great and small, are as letters to make us ponder the invisible things of God." This long tradition of spiritualists might be called the Footprintists, those who understood that our holiest work is "studying in minute detail the foot-prints of God in the world," as ecotheologian Belden Lane put it in *Ravished by Beauty*, his 2011 study of the historical development—from John Calvin to Jonathan Edwards—of a sensual theology of beauty and desire.

Think not that it's straightforward business. Nor an obvious read.

"The book of nature is like a page written over or printed upon with different-sized characters and in many different languages, interlined and cross-lined, and with a great variety of marginal notes and references," observed John Burroughs, the inimitable Hudson Valley essayist who subscribed to a quiet, close-to-home approach to nature watching. "There is coarse print and fine print; there are obscure signs and hieroglyphics. . . . It is a book which he reads best who goes most slowly or even tarries long by the way."

Nature, always protagonist but often antagonist of the eponymous Book, is not one to billboard its secrets.

In an essay titled "The Art of Seeing Things," Burroughs continues: "So far as seeing things is an art, it is the art of keeping your eyes and ears open. The art of nature is all in the direction of concealment. The birds, the animals, all the wild creatures, for the most part try to elude your observation. The art of the bird is to hide her nest; the art of the game you are in quest of is to make itself invisible."

For our purposes, the game of which Burroughs writes is a hide-and-seek of the holy variety. Not only are the sightings elusive, demanding of urgent attention—a quick eye, a steady gaze, the patience of an Assisian Francis— the scrollwork of creation tends to be fine-grained, subtle. Which is why its disciples—those seers and saints who've authored the literature of illumination on creation's manuscript, a trove populated by the likes of Barry Lopez, Terry Tempest Williams, J. Drew Lanham, Annie Dillard, and Thomas Merton, to name just a few illuminati from not-distant decades—have proven themselves indispensable. They point the way toward deeper reading.

"I became a student of subtle differences: the way a breeze may flutter a single leaf on a whole tree, leaving the other leaves silent and unmoved (had not that leaf, then, been brushed by a magic?); or the way the intensity of the sun's heat expresses itself in the precise rhythm of the crickets," writes David Abram, in his lyrical *The Spell of the Sensuous*, drawing from Balinese shamanism, Apache storytelling, and his own past as a sleight-of-hand prestidigitator, to reawaken us to the language of this holy earth.

It might be fleeting and furtive, but it's not in short supply, the Book of Creation's wild-grace wisdoms. In the words of Dillard, who penned that paean to paying attention, *Pilgrim at Tinker Creek*, "The world is fairly studded and strewn with pennies cast broadside from a generous hand."

Indeed, it's worth pausing here to consider one of the great origin stories magnifying the penny-strewn nature of all creation, one drawn from ancient Judaic mysticism, underscoring how all the cosmos came to be consecrated or filled with sparks of the divine. It's known as the Mystery of the Shattering or Splintering of the Vessels; in Hebrew, *Shevirah*. And it goes like this:

At the beginning of time, God's presence filled the universe. When God decided to make heaven and earth, God drew in a breath, which made the darkness. When God said, "Let there be light," a light thus filled the darkness, and ten holy vessels appeared, each filled with this first breath or primordial light. God then sent forth those vessels, like a fleet of sanctified ships, each ferrying its cargo of light. But the vessels were too fragile for such a luminous heavenly light, and so the vessels shattered or splintered and holy sparks rained down "like sand, like seeds, like stars," as one especially beautiful telling puts it. The sparks fell everywhere, onto and into everything. And that's why, according to the myth, we humans were created: to gather up the sparks, no matter where hidden. It is our holy task to be spark seekers. When enough shards of holiness have been gathered, when the vessels are restored, then *tikkun olam*, the repair of the world, long awaited, will be complete.

Our paying attention, then, our seeking the sparks of holiness within and under and over and through all of creation, it's not some dalliance or diversion. We're not strapping on our hiking shoes, fetching our butterfly nets for the pure frolic of it. We're getting about the business of infusing ourselves—and the broken world all around—with all the holiness we can muster. We are called to attention and witness. Who knows what you'll find lurking there on the edge of some murky old pond?

It's the cloud of unknowing we're aiming to lift with our curiosities piqued and our inquisitions endless. Dillard elucidates: "We remove the veils one by one, painstakingly, adding knowledge to knowledge and whisking away veil after veil, until at last we reveal the nub of things, the sparkling equation from whom all blessings flow."

It's the nub—that holy, holy nub—that I seek.

In truth, it won't take long to amass a veritable catalog of astonishments, should we pay attention to what mythologist Martin Shaw calls "the trembling mysteries," to follow the call of that late great rabbi and thinker Abraham Joshua Heschel, who implored that we "live life in radical amazement, get up in the morning and look at the world in a way that takes nothing for granted. . . . To be spiritual is to be amazed."

The point of all this watchkeeping is that it can't help but train our sights on the crosshairs of wonder in our everyday. To drench us in the undeniable beauties of God, the ones reminding us how infinitesimal we are against the immensities of heaven, and how unendingly God delights in sharing the holiest romp with us all. And isn't the point of this very close reading to come to the closest knowledge of God through the very intricacies poured onto each page of the vast Book of Nature?

A necessary exercise in probing that genius, I find, is to peel away the apparent, to reach for the marvels of science undergirding it all. It's the utter brilliance, spelled out in the laws of botany or physics, in astronomical algorithms and mathematical formulas, in the uncanny repetitions of ubiquitous patterns and shapes—the golden ratio, the spiral, the circle, the hexagon, the whorls and ellipses and fractals, even plain old spots and stripes—that to me seals the deal on the Great Intelligence.

I'm hardly alone in my inclination to lean into science, specifically as a factor in multiplying the holy. Here's Robert Macfarlane on the late great wilderness writer Lopez, who seriously considered becoming a Trappist monk or a priest before devoting his writing life to the wilds and authoring his 1986 masterpiece *Arctic Dreams*, among a catalog of great works:

"Lopez's scientific training [as a field biologist] also helped him. Through it, he came to realize the importance of fact as a carrier of wonder," wrote Macfarlane. "*Arctic Dreams* is packed with data: about the crystallography of frazil ice, or the thermodynamics of polar-bear hair.. ... Science, for Lopez, finesses the real into a greater marvelousness. Arctic mirages were once thought to be the work of angels; they are now known to be the work of angles. For Lopez, the two are never far apart."

How then do we come to see in such fine-grained texture and intricacy, fix our lens on what the lyrical Williams refers to as "wild nature's seasonal fugue of infinite composition and succession"?

Frederick Buechner, a seer if ever there was, sets no low bar here: "Look with Rembrandt's eye, listen with Bach's ear, look with X-ray eyes that see beneath the surface to whatever lies beneath the surface." There's a difference, he's reminding us, and what we're after is the deep-down noticing, a sacramental attention. Shaw, the mythologist, makes clear: "There's a difference between seeing something and beholding it."

Begin by stalking. "You have to stalk everything," Dillard insists. Otherwise it's only a glimpse, and you're likely to miss it altogether.

This paying attention in such up-close scale, and hot on the trail of catching the divine in the act, insists on patience. "No one knows when God will choose to reveal himself," reminded Welsh poet and Anglican priest R. S. Thomas, who said he was sometimes more apt to notice God's exit than entrance or presence, too often feeling "the draught that was God leaving." Merton, the monk of Gethsemani, who read deeply and ecumenically the wisdoms of multiple spiritual disciplines—Christian Desert Fathers, Taoist philosophers, Buddhist Zen masters, and more—reminds us "not to run from one thought to next." Rather, give each thought "time to settle in the heart."

The Japanese embrace the ancient knowing of *hakanasa*, or evanescence, best expressed in veneration toward the cherry blossom. Its beauty, the Zen masters teach, is all the more piercing because it won't last; any minute a breeze might blow and the petals will flutter to earth, a pink-tinged perfumed rain. God has made everything beautiful for its time; the abbreviations only serve to intensify.

While wisdom seekers across time have turned their gaze, their beholding, to the whole of the cosmos, it is a watchkeeping infused deep into the DNA of two particular tribes, ones now braided into my own ecology of awe: the Jews and the Celts, both rooted in the humus and the turning of this holy earth, and whose prayers and praise resound with the vernacular of star and moon, sea and sod, rain and drought, seed and season.

In Hebrew, *Sim lev!*—the command form of "pay attention"—literally means "put forth your heart." It's the call to divine attention especially. And it's one that's long echoed among the people of Israel, a summons across time and timelessness for all who are keen to the holy call. It's a sacred thread sewn through all of Jewish history. In the Warsaw ghetto, the Hasidic rabbi Kalonymus Kalman Shapira taught a form of meditation called *hashkatah*, or quieting, of which a central element was honing a "sensitization to holiness," a process of discovering the holiness within oneself and the natural world. Martin Buber, the Austrian-Israeli philosopher, distilled the sacred purpose into three simple words, one blessed truth: "hallow the everyday."

The Celts, another ancient rural people, this time from the unforgiving rugged lands anchored in the Irish Sea and the North Atlantic, lived by the same simple code. They too listened for God—"the Lord of the Elements"— in all things, and recognized the world as a place of revelation, the whole of life as sacramental. It's been said that the first cathedral of worship to the Celts was all that unspooled under God's holy dome. They were a people who asked, as in an eighteenth-century Welsh poem, "How many bright wonders does this world contain . . . how many mirrors of His finest work offer themselves a hundred times to our gaze?" And the soulful response of these sea-faring, field-toiling, flock-herding folk, who lived by the tides and the seasons' turning, highly attuned to the laws and the language of nature: to attend and to bless each stitch of the day with *beannacht* (Gaelic for "benediction" or "blessing"). Theirs was a life of ceaseless prayer rooted in the quotidian, from kindling the morning fire to milking the cow and planting the seed, to spying the moon and smoldering the day's last embers.

"These are the prayers of a people who have so much to do from dawn to dusk from dark to dark, that they had little time for long, formal prayers," explains Celtic scholar Esther de Waal, of the elemental prayers gathered in Gaelic in an extraordinarily beautiful compendium, *Carmina Gadelica*. It's a collection of incantations, hymns, blessings, and charms recorded mostly in the Gaelic-speaking Outer Hebrides of Scotland between 1860 and 1909 by a folklorist, Alexander Carmichael, who surely saved a treasure from the ash bin of history.

It was believed by these imaginal people from a place of wind-swept moors and craggy mounds that a "thread of glory" wove through the warp and weft of all creation's tapestry.

Much like the tight focus of Japanese haiku, or the sure brush of the Impressionist painter, the Celtic way of prayer was especially attentive to so subtle a thing as shadow and nuance of color. Not an iota of grace was taken for granted. Echoing the ancient Hebrews' tie to their Holy Land, the Celts held an astonishing confidence that God had showered them with blessings, and through their simple anointing of each and all, theirs was a praise song always rising.

This call to attention, as prescribed and practiced by Celts or Jews, Zen Buddhists or Shinto priests, modern-day popes or medieval mystics, is quite simply our surest hope of hewing to Meister Eckhart's admonition to "learn to penetrate things and find God there."

In the opening passage of his classic work *The Human Phenomenon*, Pierre Teilhard de Chardin spelled out the imperative: "*Seeing.* One could say that the whole of life lies in seeing—if not ultimately, at least essentially. . . . That is probably why the history of the living world can be reduced to the elaboration of ever more perfect eyes at the heart of a cosmos where it is always possible to discern more. . . . To try to see more and to see better is not, therefore, just a fantasy, curiosity, or a luxury. See or perish."

It's either or, to be blunt. If the Book of Nature is the text we're longing to read, to bump up against the One who breathed it and penned it, then the one holy practice, the necessary practice, is that of paying attention. Only then might we see: the seen and the unseen, all of it, all along the road to epiphany, where attention points the way.

Nothing is more essential to prayer than attentiveness.

—Evagrius the Solitary, fourth-century monk and ascetic

PAGES FROM THE BOOK OF NATURE

The meditations in the pages to come are prayerful immersions into the earthly kaleidoscope where the sacred awaits—but there pulses through each an awareness that, as a planet, we are teetering on a very thin edge: this blessed creation, the whole of it, is in peril. If the wilds—the water's edge, the woods, the humble stirrings in our own backyards—are the places to which we retreat to encounter the divine, then to lose even a shard of those wilds—to fire, to drought, to pestilence, to flood—is to cut ourselves off from the holy font.

In many ways, these meditations are paeans to the astonishments of all creation and to the Creator. Beneath their ponderings each is a prayer.

Yet prayer is raw as often as it is undiluted praise. True prayer isn't gauzy; it wields a sharp edge. True prayer doesn't avert its gaze.

If we can't hear the lament of the milkweed for the monarch, if we don't mourn the drying up of the wetlands, or the extinction of the ivory-billed woodpecker, we are turning away from God's loneliest dirge.

And we're ignoring a profound invitation to action, to reparation, *through* the divine.

The radical proposition is this: to notice, to offer our apt gaze and even our goosebumps, is to begin to partake of the holy work, to answer the call not merely to dance in the whirl of creation but to work toward its salvation. The time for inattention is past.

At heart, this is a book of wonder. As you read, though, you might consider how wonder so often entails lament—an aching for what we might lose, even before it's lost. It's a spiritual reading meant to heighten our seeing, our belief that nothing less than the sacred is at stake.

In the Book of Nature I read, God comes in a thousand thousand guises. In the spacious music of silence, as I stand in the shadow of an ancient star. In the muffled footfall of the night critters rustling the winter garden. In the first filigree of dawn's light as it drapes onto the form of the one who sleeps beside me. It is all a beckoning.

In the Book of Nature I read, God comes in a thousand thousand guises. These are a few of its pages. . . .

THE EARTHLY

THE EARTHLY

GARDEN

Of all the chapters in my own well-thumbed, dog-eared copy of the Book of Nature, the one I read most assiduously, on my knees more often than not, is the one that falls from the humble plot of my own swatch of earth, my gardens secret and otherwise. I read its pages as if by Braille, through the whorl of my fingertips—plunged into loam, rubbing granules or velvety leaf or curlicue of cucumber vine—in marvel and astonishment at the way it all works, following rules as old as time, defying all sense.

To tend a garden, to keep close watch on the rise and fall of the rhythms of earth and its dance with the sun, is to enter into the frailties and absurdities, the puzzles and conundrums that elude reason or rhyme. Or so it seems in the crushing hours, the ones a gardener alone might suffer, wincingly so, when a hyacinth you've awaited all spring is scythed at the stalk by a possum or skunk digging for heaven knows what. Or a storm blows through in the night and you awake to a broken-off limb that's taken out the lilac you planted ages ago, a rescue from your grandmother's long-razed gardens. But just as certainly, the lessons might be drawn from the gospel of resilience, told in the verse of the morning glory that bloomed well past the autumn's first frost. And sometimes the garden is preaching resurrection, when you all but tag a gnarly old vine for dead, and a first bit of green unfurls and you realize you're back in business again. It's give-and-take, in both directions. There've been nights when frost warnings flashed on the 10 o'clock news, and I've dashed out the door with a brigade of blankets and beach towels to save my tenderlings from the indecent incoming freeze. And there've been spells when my garden should have given up on me, what with the ways I've ignored it, caught up in the weight of my worries and the tasks that burden the hours. Yet the stubborn old plot, the one that will not succumb, it lures me back, bejewels me, with some spectacular bloom, or a heavenly scent that sends me swooning, straight over the moon. It's been decades now, the tango of me and my garden. We've grown into each other. And we've both grown.

Sometimes I almost sense God as the master gardener, taking me, the fumbling acolyte, hand-in-hand along the perennial border, pausing to point my otherwise-scattered attention to this little wonder or that. And then, because I've been beguiled by beauty or scent or simply the force of some little green thing's wily resolve to stick its neck out, I move in for close inspection; I see now as never before, now that I see through the Book of Nature's overlay, that this is all a line or verse or page from God's unspoken text. I know now that even in my hardly praiseworthy plot, where I sometimes forget to turn off the hose or leave unattended some trespassing vine, there rises aplenty divine wisdom and wonder. And oughtn't I follow the syllabus?

Take, for instance, one late summer's delphinium, its primal scream of cobalt calling to me from its improbable ascension, squeezed between a rock and a rain spout. It's the color that beckons. But then, as I fold myself in for a closer look, my mind carries me off to that netherworld of godly considerations: the inexplicability of how, some two hundred million years ago, there blossomed out of unimaginable nothingness a botanical triumph, a world suddenly carpeted in the wildest of flowers, an evolutionary revolution that all these millennia later has led to this unlikely larkspur (the common name for the stalk with the dolphin-shaped flowers) I now behold. Even the evolutionist Charles Darwin termed it "an abominable mystery," the unfurling of sepal and petal, the bloom of seduction. I drift further on: the reproductive calculus of wind and itty-bitty grain of pollen, smaller than the dot of a lower-case i. Or the long-tongued bumblebees and folded-wing butterflies who enter the dance, on whose appendages the delphinium depends for a slim chance at survival. It's somewhere deep in that mystery where the clarion gong goes off. The mental gymnastics it takes to even begin to fathom such slim-to-none odds. How could this be, if not for one almighty God? And if so exquisite an omniscience lies at the essence of a nearly forgotten back-garden bloom, then how much, how intently, must our God have considered when ideating little old us?

And then, too, there are the visceral epiphanies—how, after a long night's rainy deluge, when I embark on morning rounds, assessing casualties, gathering the wounded, and find myself cradling a broken-necked peony in my sturdy palms, I catch a sudden glimpse of how God so cradles me in my own hours of brokenness. Absorbing the sting of this now-ruptured stalk, a tear soon spills. Not only because I'm crushed to lose what would have been, the lacy mop of tissue-paper pink and white, but because I can't shake the piercing sense of how God, too, might hurt when God spies me banged-up and askew on the days when I lose my way.

Such are the mind leaps that now infuse my hours in the garden, as if I'm always on alert for the hide-and-seek of where the lessons lie. It's as if my trowel and twine are necessary tools for godly revelation. And what I pluck now from my garden never ever wilts.

The garden, of course, is just about the oldest metaphor in the holy book. It's where it all began, at least in the Bible. In the thick of creation, God reached right down, and from a handful of dust there on the ground—*adamah*, in Hebrew—God made Adam, so there'd be someone to tend the acreage. And then God planted the garden, and put Adam there "to till it and keep it." And ever since, we've been tilling and keeping the earth. Or aiming to, anyways. It doesn't seem like God ever abandons the garden. And you get the sense pretty quick that it's there for more than simply delight. You get the sense, reading all the sages and saints, that God wants us in the garden to learn a thing or two. Sometimes I think God likes to spell out wisdoms in pistils and stamens and rhizomes and roots, there's so much to reap there. Francis of Assisi, a saint incomprehensibly in sync with the earth's sacred whispers, "asked that part of the friary garden always be left untouched, so that the wild flowers and herbs could grow there, and those who saw them could raise their minds to God, the creator of such beauty." So reminded Pope Francis in his 2015 encyclical *Laudato Si*, on caring for this blessed globe, in which he turned to his medieval namesake for sacred instruction against the threat of a deeply wounded Mother Earth.

At the end of the nineteenth century, Thérèse of Lisieux read, too, from the garden, gleaning insights from what bloomed behind the walls of her nunnery. In a letter to her prioress in 1897, she confided the story of how she named herself Jesus's Little Flower:

> He opened the book of nature before me, and I saw that every flower He has created has a beauty of its own, that the splendor of the rose and the lily's whiteness do not deprive the violet of its scent nor make less ravishing the daisy's charm. I saw that if every little flower wished to be a rose, Nature would lose her spring adornments, and the fields would be no longer enameled with their varied flowers. So it is in the world of souls, the living garden of the Lord. It pleases him to create great Saints, who may be compared with the lilies or the rose; but He has also created the little ones, who must be content to be daisies or violets, nestling at His feet to delight his eyes when He should choose to look at them.

Oh, that I might remember in my own hours of littleness, of feeling "less than" in a world of seemingly endless bigness and boldness, that my quiet little violet of a self is more than enough.

In 1616, Thomas Adams, known as "the Shakespeare of the English Puritans," published a series of five sermons on the spiritual lessons to be learned from herbs in English gardens, a tome titled *A Divine Herball, Together with a Forrest of Thornes*. In his preface to the Earl of Pembroke, to whom the sermons were presented, Adams pointed out—for reasons culinary or otherwise, it's unclear—that those herbs were "cut in rough pieces," as opposed perhaps to fine mince. Another who found religion in the flower beds was the great Jesuit poet Gerard Manley Hopkins, particularly keen on English bluebells, of which he declared, "I know the beauty of our Lord by it." The reason, he explained in his 1870 journal, was its "overhung neck." Turns out he was keen for any botanicals—catkins, ash key, bluebells—that "hang their heads, as

Christ hangs his head on the cross in medieval paintings," an unlikely botanical attraction recounted by the late British naturalist Roger Deakin in his 2007 wonderwork *Wildwood*. I shall ne'er see a bluebell quite the same again.

I'll confess that I didn't always find religion out where the grass isn't meant to grow and the dandelions do their darnedest to seize eminent domain. When I was a wee little rascal, and found my way into mischief, I wasn't sent to my room; I was sent out to weed. It was penance with pointy-edged digger. And, over the years, I've pretty much annihilated every houseplant that's been under my watch. But not long after my husband, Blair, and I married, when we bought our first house, a sun-drenched Victorian I miss to this day, it came with a tiny, lovingly tended, fenced-in garden, a garden so meticulously planted with twisty trees in miniature and blooms that arose in choreographed succession, I came to think of it as my petit-point tapestry, and it drew me to my knees. Before it was ours, I stopped by one day to peek around, and I heard the wails of the gardener who was leaving it behind. That's a keening you never forget. So, once it *was* ours, I picked up my trowel with a weighty sense of both duty and devotion. I struck a taproot, all right, and something holy started to flow. In *me*. That garden—where a priest, a rabbi, and a tight circle of people we love gathered for blessings shortly after the births of each of our boys; where baby bunnies and nestlings and goldfish were buried after premature deaths; where our stubbornly resistant house cat mastered the art of escape—that plat of earth became as sacred to me as any cloister garth.

Not only was it where I knelt to teach my firstborn the magic of tucking a spit-out watermelon seed into the loam and, each morning after, tracking its implausible surge. During seven long years of miscarriage after miscarriage, ectopic pregnancy and emergency surgery, and doctors finally telling us to give up hope, I dug and I dug in that garden, all but willing the tiniest bulbs and tenderest sprouts to beat impossible odds, refusing to let anything else die on my watch. And then, at the end of one summer, as the crab apples were starting to turn, a rabbi who lived down the block came by with his wife, whom I'd long called my fairy gardenmother for her magical ways and her unbroken guidance. Standing under the stars, the rabbi, his wife, and I, we blessed the garden itself, casting prayers and sprinklings of water. By that Christmas, I was pregnant, with nary a drop of medical intervention. Just shy of forty-five when that blessing of a baby arrived the next August, I've always wondered if maybe the rabbi mixed up the garden fertility prayers.

It's all a holy whirl—that intricate and inseparable interweaving that is the cosmos.

Francis Thompson, a late-nineteenth-century English poet, once mused that you can't pluck a flower without troubling a star, though he dipped into the Victorian inkwell, penning it thusly: "That thou canst not stir a flower / Without troubling of a star." The whole of creation's garden—from the intricately chiseled seedcases that catch on the fur of a passing-by fox, to weightless thistledown riding the wind, to the abounding acres of sunflowers that once nearly lured me off the blue highways of Michigan's countryside when I took the crooked way home—is genius endlessly, endlessly scripted.

And the seed, in my book, holds enough theology to carry me a plenty long while. George Bernard Shaw once wrote, "Think of the fierce energy concentrated in an acorn! You bury it in the ground, and it explodes into a giant oak! Bury a sheep, and nothing happens but decay." There's a children's book, *The Carrot Seed* by Ruth Krauss, in which a little boy silently ignores all the doubters and deniers who insist his tiny carrot seed won't amount to anything. Undaunted, he patiently waters and weeds his little seed, until at last the triumphant seedling emerges, "just as the little boy had known it would." A story of faith, if ever there was. And, as biologist Thor Hanson writes in *The Triumph of Seeds*, his examination of how grains, nuts, kernels, and pips (all seeds, by definition) conquered the plant kingdom and shaped human history: "Even children know that the tiniest pip contains what George Bernard Shaw called 'fierce energy'—the spark and all the instructions needed to build a carrot, an oak tree, wheat, mustard, sequoias, or any one of the 353,000 other kinds of plants that use seeds to reproduce."

It's mighty hard not to believe, when tucking in a seed, sprinkling it day after day with your watering can, and catching sight, glorious sight, of that first hint of newborn green pushing through the earth. To plant a seed, to bury a bulb, is to practice resurrection gardening. And to watch in real time how faith works. Some of us need to rub it between our fingertips, to get its dirt stuck under our nails.

If you'd do well to stumble on a sign of something sacred, look no further than the miracle of the seed birthed in the inferno, a rising-from-the-dead story that's played out in the wake of history's darkest hours. Most famous is the story of the seeds of Hiroshima, when in the aftermath of the atomic fireball in August of 1945, the city staggered through never-before-witnessed devastation. As survivors scrounged for unburned rubble to try to patch together homes, word came from a prominent physician that nothing would grow there for seventy years, with all flora and fauna incinerated across a five-mile swath. Barely a month after the bombing, though, rising from the charred bits, less than half a mile from the explosion's radioactive center, red canna lilies and delicate wildflowers began to sprout and bloom amid the wasteland. In his classic 1946 account of Hiroshima in the *New Yorker*, John Hersey indelibly describes it:

> The bomb had not only left the underground organs of plants intact; it had stimulated them. Everywhere were bluets and Spanish bayonets, goosefoot, morning glories and day lilies, the hairy-fruited bean, purslane and clotbur and sesame and panic grass and feverfew. Especially in a circle at the center, sickle senna grew in extraordinary regeneration, not only standing among the charred remnants of the same plant but pushing up in new places, among bricks and through cracks in the asphalt. It actually seemed as if a load of sickle-senna seed had been dropped along with the bomb.

What had happened, in part, was that the bricks of Hiroshima had been formed of clay from the mountains, where wildflowers grew. Walls throughout the city secretly had been harboring long dormant seeds. And in the cataclysm of the bomb, the explosive power split open the seeds, and the mountain flowers sprouted. Out of horror, erupted beauty. Ever since, the survivor seeds of Hiroshima have been revered in Japan, as "the faith that grew out of the ashes."

I wish I'd known when I last walked the meandering lanes of London that three centuries before Hiroshima's atomic bomb, in the spring of 1667, Londoners who'd endured the Great Fire six months before, watched in amazement as their singed city burst into bloom, with fields of golden mustard and other wildflowers sweeping north from the River Thames. The fire, which razed thousands of homes, had exposed bare ground and a seed bank buried for decades and decades. Again, it's a phoenix story spelled out in seed, the original indomitable sanctum of impending blossoming. It enthralls me plenty.

No wonder I take my religion so often with trowel in hand. Have consecrated so many cubic yards with my tears, in jubilation, epiphany, or sorrow— the earth to which I'm pulled when words escape me.

WOODS

There is a secret patch of woods by my house that had eluded me for years. I discovered it, of course, only by accident; walking by one autumn day, when the sumacs were blazing blood red, I noticed an ash tree akimbo. It appeared a woody tangle had been shoved to the side, and beyond it, a path had been trod hardly discernibly. I caught the whiff of mischief, a scent that has not yet been solved (though the evidence, in the scatterings left in the woods—a chair here, half a mannequin there, a wide-screen TV monitor teetering atop a tree trunk, and, one day, a tepee—bolsters my case by the week).

Bending nearly in half to keep from banging my forehead, I slipped in, enchanted from first footfall. There was the forest light, for starters, dappled and filtered and falling in sprees, checkerboard patches of shadow and sun-beam all over the leafy plush-piled floor. Once through an allée of natural making, with saplings that seemed to reach across the aisle, the vault opened into a suddenly airy enclosure of trees with sky for the faraway ceiling. It's one of the oldest architecture tricks in the book, the one preached by that high priest of compress-and-release, Frank Lloyd Wright, who borrowed most of his tricks from the woods of his Wisconsin youth. This sylvan nave in which I found myself is one I've come to think of as Leviathan's Toy Chest, for the uncanny assemblage of tree stumps—toppled and otherwise—that seem to have spilled, goliathan building blocks in a goliathan's nursery. A friendly giant, I'd imagine. It's a place, from the start, that invited me in to play. It's high on my places-to-pray list, as holy a place as any into which

I've tumbled—or maybe I've trespassed—a tabernacle tucked under the trees. Unlike the mischievous woodsfolk who leave behind their playthings, I am hushed to a whisper here and I behave with impeccable church-person decorum. I do not disturb. Mostly I sit and watch and listen. "Trees are sanctuaries," wrote Hermann Hesse in a 1920 collection titled *Wandering: Notes and Sketches*. "Whoever knows how to speak to them, whoever knows how to listen to them, can learn the truth. They do not preach learning and precepts, they preach, undeterred by particulars, the ancient law of life." I come to the woods for that preaching.

Woods have a way of slowing you down. The labyrinth of tree roots snaking along underfoot stand ready to make a good day's orthopedic repair of you and your ankles, should you not pay attention. Chandeliers of unidentified disco-pink petals and vines dangling from boughs like a dead man's cord threaten to catch you by the neck if you're not watching. The place is awash in the oddest of soundtracks; sometimes it's Hitchcockian haunting. I'd not known that old arthritic trees creak like masts of a weathered old vessel, or a bentwood rocker left out in the rain. It's a sound that can make you glance over your shoulder, eyes extra-wide, on the lookout for trouble. The wind, too, is an instrument of a thousand sounds, as it harps through the leaves, and turns the grasses to whistles. Sometimes, though, it's so quiet you can just barely hear a leaf make its soft landing. And then the woodpecker picks up the tempo, banging away at his incessant construction.

With every shift of the season or weather, the kaleidoscope turns just a tad (sometimes head-spinningly so), and there are new things to see and to study: in the striptease of fall and the ornamenting of spring, when in delicate, delicate filigree and uprisings of all-new color, the woods burst back to life, you can hardly keep up. In the thick of the summer and the bare-naked winter, when all is exposed, each trek to the woods begs up-close inspection. The sky alone is a slideshow in saturations and striations, the blues and the grays, and the insertions of cloud in every which accumulation. Lichens and moss could bewitch you all day, so too the trail of a snail making its house under a fungus. I've spent whole hours running my fingers up and down the reptilian bark of various trees; one reminds of an alligator, another a wrinkled-hide lizard. And then there's the archeology of decay, as old timbers tumble and rot. That's when you notice there's not a rectilinear trunk in the place, it's all crooked or cockeyed or bent; makes me think God is lacking a straight-edge.

It wouldn't be false to say I grew up in the woods. Though not in a Thoreauvian way. I grew up in old suburbia, in a house with five kids, an ad man of a dad who carried a briefcase and came home, religiously, every night on the 6:20 train, and a stay-at-home mom whose prized possession might have been her optical-grade binoculars, the ones she took to the window or the woods when anything winged fluttered by. By the time we moved into our house under an arbor of oaks, the old orphanage next door had been taken over by a somewhat laissez-faire family of ten kids, two Great Danes, a rooster named Rudy (he ruled the stockade fence that ran between our yards), a never-quite-documented number of kittens and cats, a goldfish pond, and a greenhouse filled with dried-up Christmas poinsettias and Easter azaleas.

Just the other side of the street, up the banks from the creek where the crawfish hid under rocks, were my woods. The woods where I did all my best thinking. The woods where I imagined myself in my very own little house on the prairie, a larder filled with honeysuckle berries and acorns. My best friend Martha and I had one particular log for the deepest of thinks, like the day we awaited the birth of my littlest brother (I have four). Martha's mother never minded when we'd raid the refrigerator, and haul our stash to the log, so we never went hungry there in the woods where we knew not to walk on the rarest of trillium. And besides, I could always hear the gong of my mother's cast-iron dinner bell so I could scamper home to meatloaf, mashed potatoes, and peas by 6:25, religiously.

Nowadays, the woods are where I go to get lost. Not lost in a geographical way, but lost as in away from the hard geometry of street-grid suburbia, where numbers and signs insist on pinpointing us. The paths in my woods resist the linear, celebrate the circuitous. *Wait, wasn't I here just a minute ago? Where is the trailhead to carry me home?* I get lost with purpose.

Every once in a while, as Rebecca Solnit once wrote, we need to get lost. It's paradoxical: we get lost to find our way out. It's a conundrum that ranks as an oft-overlooked spiritual practice. How can we exercise our wayfinding selves if we never feel that quiver of panic that this might be the one time we cannot find our way to the clearing, and darkness is coming, and rainclouds are curdling, and what if the lightning does strike?

Here's the spiritual imperative pressing up against that question: Living as we do in a world of ready answers, in a world where advances in science and technology peel away mystery, in a world where Google seems to know everything, are we conditioning ourselves to never not know? Are we expelling ourselves from the realm of any uncertainty? It's a question Solnit raises in her field guide to getting lost, one she poses through a translation said to come from Plato's fictional philosopher Meno, in one of the *Dialogues*: "How will you go about finding that thing the nature of which is totally unknown to you?"

It's "the basic tactical question in life," writes Solnit, and one on which she muses: "Love, wisdom, grace, inspiration—how do you go about finding these things that are in some ways about extending the boundaries of the self into unknown territory?"

I'd add to that list, *God*.

How do we go about finding God if we stick to what's known, and dread the unknown? If we're not willing to extend our boundaries beyond the familiar? Insist always on proof? The poets urge us, as did John Keats, to exercise our capacities "of being in uncertainties, Mysteries, doubts, without any irritable reaching after fact and reason." The God we seek doesn't come with proofs, God comes by way of the ephemeral, ineffable.

It is good, every once in a while, to simply roam. To poke around with nothing but a double dose of curiosity, and—especially in a digital age when we're leashed to our smartphones—the rare luxury of not only timelessness but placelessness. I admit to not unleashing myself often enough from my to-do lists and my smartphone reminders (I nearly always set the maximum three alerts; I'd likely set six if I could). Not having an agenda, not knowing where we are in the woods, might acquaint us with unknowing. Might teach us to breathe easier at the edge of mystery. Might coax us just a little bit closer into a landscape where doubt and uncertainty rough the terrain.

When I apply the lessons of the woods, the practices of the pathfinder to my God quest, I am rooting myself in surrendering posture. I don't know quite where I'm going, or where and what I will find. But the willingness to enter the thicket, uncertain of how I'll find my way home, is to find my place in a mindset where proof is beyond reach, and hardly a hindrance to the beauties I find along the way.

The particular woods where I now lose and find my way have been here at least a century, ever since metropolitan planners—aghast at filth and foul water, and eager to flush a down-yonder river—decided to hollow out a meandering stream that ran along the woods' edge to make way for a canal. Though technically a sanitary chute that controls the flow of floodwater and muck into and out of Lake Michigan, just around the bend to the east, I pretend it's merely a slow-stirring river. And, besides, through the copse of trees, pretending is a cinch. The trees in the woods can play it both ways: they can hide or reveal; they're a scrim or a lightbox.

"The trees are innately holy," pronounces biologist Colin Tudge in *The Secret Life of Trees*. Groves of redwoods, Tudge writes, are often compared to the naves of great cathedrals, and a single banyan tree, with its multitude of trunks, is like a temple or mosque. But the metaphor, he insists, should be pointed the opposite way. The cathedrals and mosques find their roots in God's forests, the vaults and living colonnades that rise from the earth.

In the Book of Nature, as told in God's follow-up text, the Book of the Word, the tree steps into the very first act, right there in Genesis 2:9, the tree of life in the midst of the garden of Eden, and the tree of the knowledge of good and evil. And again, at the cymbal-crashing climax of the last chapter of Revelation, on either side of the river of life, there grows the tree of life with its twelve kinds of fruit, the original fruit of the month, and its leaves "for the healing of nations." There is but one other protagonist tree in the Scriptures, and that, of course, is the tree of the crucifixion, thought in some legends to have been a rowan tree, with berries that look to be droplets of blood. In Scotland, though, it was long thought that the tree to which Jesus was nailed, and upon which he died, was the aspen, so crofters refused to use its wood for any farm tool or fishing rod. It's this notion of contrition that pulses behind a line from an old Gaelic poem: "Hence the ever-tremulous, ever-quivering, ever-quaking motion of the guilty hateful aspen in the stillest air." According to lore said to have "come down the long stream of time," passersby hurled clods of dirt and stone and curses at the guilt-riddled tree. Such pummeling of any tree in reputation and form is the exception. Yet somehow it underscores the ancient interplay of the texts of creation and Scripture, and how something deeper than sense drives our reading of each.

Sometimes, when closely reading the Book of Nature, the profoundest of lessons are learned from the quietest, most quotidian of happenstance. Suddenly seeing what you might have walked past countless dozens of times. Being awake to gospel in the plainest of wrappers. A buck-naked tree, perhaps. A tree whose very nakedness suddenly offers *aha!*

Brother Lawrence, the seventeenth-century barefoot friar who found God in the pots and the pans of his monastery kitchen in Paris, told one such story. In his one published work, a collection of fourteen letters, a wisp of an eighty-page volume I once unearthed from a library's musky archives, he wrote how a tree in winter, stripped of its leaves, played the pivotal role in his uncanny conversion. It seems the good brother absorbed the tree's stark emptiness, and, in that way that saints and wise souls do, he saw beyond it. He imagined the possible. As it's recorded in his little book's preface, the soon-to-be friar stood before the naked tree picturing its branches soon filled with tiny leaves as if clasped in prayer. And thus he was hit, head-on. The surging sense of the immensity of the Holy One all but knocked him down, realizing the life force, the beautiful that would burst from the barren. In his little book's preface, I was struck most of all by how strange it is that divine attributes can sometimes be seen in something so common. And how we'll miss the whole of it if we refuse to be stopped in our tracks. I sighed in recognition when I read, "It is rather to be wondered at, that others are not affected as [Brother Lawrence] was, and that the little miracles of nature make so little impression upon us."

It's my aim here to crank up my impressionability.

I'm hardly alone. Reverence for trees is blessedly woven in and through myriad traditions. The Japanese, who make a healing art of forest bathing, *shinrin-yoku*, name their pine trees *matsu*, which translates to "waiting for a god's soul to descend from heaven," and the Japanese cedar is believed to be the landmark for deities who visit on festival days. Special doctors, certified only after passing a fourteen-day exam issued by the Japanese government, care for old weak trees throughout the archipelago. Bashō, the haiku master, considered the chestnut "a holy tree," and walked hundreds of miles across Japan to see the famous pine of Shiogoshi. Chinese woodsmen of the T'ang and S'ung dynasties would bow to a tree before they felled it, offering a promise that it would be put to good use. In ancient Rome, the sycamore was honored by watering its roots with the finest of wines. Xerxes the Great, the war-hungry fourth king of kings of the Achaemenid Empire, "halted his unwieldy army for days that he might contemplate to his satisfaction" the beauty of one such sycamore. The Maori down under bring wooden sculptures to trees deep in the forest. Potawatomi, the people who first stalked the woods by my house, would leave a prayer and tobacco at the stub of a black ash tree after it "consented" to being chopped down for basket weaving.

All this leads me to wonder: what *are* the sermons that the woods—those places of betweenness, repositories of ancient stories—might impart from their fretwork of branches and twigs, their columnar trunks and the boughs that hold up the sky? Certainly, there are tales of resilience, the way they stand against whatever time and the weather gods hurl their way, tornado or drought, ice storm or Noah-like rains. And lessons to be learned of holy communion, the way the woods and the birds and the scampering critters all keep watch, share food, warn each other of danger, create ecosystems that moderate heat and cold, store water, and generate necessary humidity. What else of the time-tested truths, laid down like the rings revealed in a fallen tree's stump?

As I make my way through my old-growth woods, an amalgam of gnarled oaks and lopsided maples and one or two ash, I find myself wondering just how long the trees of the Leviathan's Toy Chest have been there, how many generations of wanderers and wonderers have grown up under their watch and their boughs, how long or how many timbers have surrendered themselves to those who come to this arbored acre with hatchets and axes, partaking of lumberjack practice. These woods were here before *suburbia* slipped into the American lexicon, back when William McKinley was president, and the world wars hadn't yet convulsed the globe. They must be keepers of ages-old secrets.

And maybe the reason we're drawn there is nothing more inexplicable than holiness certain and simple.

That most storied woodsman, the Transcendentalist Henry David Thoreau, saw the woods as oracular. Alone in a distant woods, he found the "equivalent to what others get by churchgoing and prayer. I come to my solitary woodland walk as the homesick go home. . . . It is as if I always met in those places some grand, serene, immortal, infinitely encouraging, though invisible, companion, and walked with him." I, too, keep watch for the woodsman's companion.

Oliver Sacks, the neurologist who kept a close eye on the nexus of natures, human and earthly, found that most sublime of arboreal attributes in one particular Micronesian rain forest: "I find myself walking softly on the rich undergrowth beneath the trees, not wanting to crack a twig, to crush or disturb anything in the least—for there is such a sense of stillness and peace that the wrong sort of movement, even one's very presence, might be felt as an intrusion." Beauty, he said, was too simple a word for what he felt there, "for being here is not just an aesthetic experience, but one steeped with mystery, and awe." My woods are a far cry from Micronesian rain forests, but I know precisely the mystery of that tabernacular silence, and every drop of the awe.

Perhaps it begins and ends with the way the trees reach toward the heavens, veiling us in a sanctuarial umbra, an ethereal presence and force the theologian Rudolf Otto termed the *mysterium tremendum*, the "awe inspiring mystery," one that at times comes "sweeping like a gentle tide pervading the mind with a tranquil mood of deepest worship." In his seminal 1917 text *The Idea of the Holy*, parsing the distinction between the numinous and the merely magical, Otto reached for the forest: "The semi-darkness that glimmers in vaulted halls, or beneath the branches of a lofty forest glade, strangely quickened and stirred by the mysterious play of half-lights, has always spoken eloquently to the soul, and the builders of temples, mosques, and churches have made full use of it."

My temple, my mosque, my church of the woods, where the center aisle is earth rubbed raw, threadbare, not unlike a great aunt's mothballed Persian rugs, where the vaulted halls are awash in shifting shadow and numinous light, bathed in a mystical halo, it is the holy place to which I return and return. It is a woods that preaches to me, fills me with wordless wisdoms. It is the place where I behold the awe-inspiring mystery of how I hope heaven will someday be.

WATER'S EDGE

I call it the place where the prayers come.

Long, long ago, the people here first named the swampy riverbed—*shikaakwa*, or, later, *Checagou*—for the stinky wild onion that grew there. They hallowed the places where earth mingled with sky, or lake waters tickled the shore, and they would have put their poetries to the name of the place not far from my house where dune grasses sway and cottonwood leaves quake in the wind, and all of it rises from hummocks of sand at the edge of the Great Lake Michigan, a word from the Ottawa elders, a word that means "great water." The people who lived here first—mostly the Potawatomi, this side of that great water—they must have had a name for this place, a name that rolled off the tongue. My name for the place is not so poetic. My name is simple: the place where the prayers come.

I am pulled there often.

It's a place that might call me at any hour; I've been there for sunrise and moonrise. I've been there on nights when there wasn't a moon to be seen. I've been there as the skies bruise to pewter then iron, the color of running for cover, when the ominous rumble grinds in the not-so distance. And I've been there during a deep freeze when the waves are caught in midcrash, and morph into mountainous bergs and ice-chiseled cliffs, when the lakescape takes on glacial proportions, the most daunting topographies here on the long-ago prairie.

More often than not, I find my seat deep in the grasses, the ones that catch the wind off the lake, and rustle much as the faithful cramped in the pews when the Sabbath comes. I nestle like quail in the rush, go as small as I can; I like to feel slight as a wisp, against a sky and a God without beginning or end. The edge of the lake, only inches away nowadays as the lake level rises, as polar ice melts, never ceases its perpetual rhythms, each with synchronous sounds: there's the quiet talk of the rare barely rippling waves, and more commonly the gurgle, the tumbling and trampling, the dialed-down roar of the lake, and on occasion, a deafening monstrous percussion—elemental cannonade—one I can hear from my house. But the sound that infuses me most, no matter the din just beyond, is the sound of quiescence—God's most necessary ingredient, perhaps.

In the place where the prayers come, the quiet is where they begin.

We come to the water's edge when what we hold cannot be contained. I remember the day my doctor called to tell me I wasn't pregnant, and likely never would be, after months and months of shots in my belly, and a morass of godawful complications, when we so wanted our firstborn not to be our one and only, in the years after we buried his unborn baby sister, the one I miscarried in the long darkness of a terrible night. I remember how I put down the phone and ran to my bike, pedaling for miles and miles along Chicago's lakefront, where the endless horizon of water and sky at last quelled my tears. I remember so sharply how in the frenzy of pedaling I made peace, praying over and over the words of my dear Blair who, as he so often does, made sense of the senseless. "We're a tiny little family," he'd told me, "but we're a marvelous little family, so let's revel in that." And the harder I rode, the more clearly I sensed that he was the mouthpiece for God. At the lake's edge, God washed me, at last, in the peace I'd sought for so long.

Is it any wonder God turned to the element of water when making our tears? Or might *this* be the wonder: When carving the earth, and filling the hollows—the seas and the ponds and even the rivulets that seep from the hillsides—God thought to pour from a vessel of tears? These are the sorts of questions that burble through my consciousness when I scan the text of creation, when I read with a God-driven purpose. When a lake is not merely a lake, nor a river a river, but rather a place in which to begin to plumb for deeper knowing. And so I keep plumbing.

While a river, a creek, and canal have places to go, the lake or the pond or even the sea is confined, its energies compounded as it surges from deep below, pulled by the invisible force of the moon. Its beauty, its fury, its form, even its color, changes from hour to hour, any one of a number of blues—lapis to turquoise to slate—"a product of one of God's blue periods, no doubt," as Belden Lane has marvelously put it. Lake Michigan rages when north winds blow, but soon as the bellows run out of breath, the great lake turns to looking glass, mirroring sky. Daniel Burnham, the master architect who laid out a plan for Chicago in 1909, knew well the gem that shimmered along the shoreline. "The Lake front by right belongs to the people," he wrote in his masterwork.

> It affords their one great unobstructed view, stretching away to the horizon, where water and clouds seem to meet. No mountains or high hills enable us to look over broad expanses of the earth's surface; and perforce we must come even to the margin of the Lake for such a survey of nature. . . . The Lake is living water, ever in motion, and ever changing in color and in the form of its waves. Across its surface comes the broad pathway of light made by the rising sun; it mirrors the ever-changing form of the clouds, and it is illumined by the glow of the evening sky. Its colors vary with the shadows that play upon it. In its every aspect it is a living thing, delighting man's eye and refreshing his spirit.

The lake then is sacramental. It's our baptismal font, and the well where we turn for absolving our sins. Literally. Each autumn, when the cottonwoods glow golden, and the air holds a tinge, during the Jewish high holy days known as the Days of Awe, we—Blair and I and our boys if they're home, as well as our rabbis and cantor, and a circle of other congregants—come to the water's edge by command. We come on the afternoon of Rosh Hashanah, the Jewish New Year, to cast our sins upon the waves. There we stand, prayerful sinners all, reciting our confessions and contritions, as we reach in our pockets and pull out great chunks of bread. It's called *taschlich*, which means "casting off" in Hebrew, and it's a ritual that began in the Middle Ages, inspired by a verse from the prophet Micah:

> He will again have compassion upon us;
> he will tread our iniquities under foot.
> You will cast all our sins
> into the depths of the sea (Mic 7:19).

It's purification for the new year unfurling, and it's the gulls' favorite day of the year, as they swoop in to pluck off our sins before they've even a minute to sponge up the lake.

I've cast my sins in plenty of waters: from the rocks along downtown Chicago's shoreline, where my first such *taschlich* had me wide-eyed and trembling, a Catholic rookie to this ancient Hebraic rite, and as we migrated north to leafy suburbs, where the same Lake Michigan still swallows our sins. One year, when we were living in Cambridge, Massachusetts, we threw our stale bread and sins into the Charles River from the iconic Weeks Footbridge, an elegant tri-span of bricks and limestone. Into the river, and on to Boston Harbor and the ocean beyond, I cast all the petty little hurts I stubbornly cling to, the flashes of fear that too often stymie me, my pent-up steam at life's injustices. A year's worth of sin drifting downriver. There is something about the constancy of the sacramental, no matter the body of water. I'm fairly convinced I could stand at the edge of a puddle and sense that God heard my confession. And my prayer of repentance.

The water's edge is a place of communion, and not only for sinners and saints. That liminal trace, the fluttering seam between land and lake, it's something of a thin blue line on the sky map, one that's been followed by migrating flocks—bird and butterfly—for ages and ages. By my house, it's the Great Lakes leg of what's called the Mississippi Flyway. Come spring or fall, when the ancestral stirring begins and the flocks take flight, south to north, north to south, depending on the season, depending where the earth's shadow falls, the night sky is thick with fluttering wings. It's a spine-tingling call to prayer when there in my grassy nook I hear the mournful cry of the goose overhead, the heaven's muezzin, flying in chevron. At the dawn, after a long night's flight, you might find the trees stippled with unseasonal color, as the rainbows of songbird land for a pause and a nibble of breakfast.

The dawn I will never forget was some years ago now, when I was walking the lake's edge, and spied first one, then another, and eventually a whole dotted line of faded-mosaic butterfly wings half-buried in the sand. The whole beach, the closer I looked, was a subtle pastiche, each left-behind wing being drained of its sunset tint, a watercolor washed out by the hour. It was a burial ground of fallen butterflies, monarchs, whose name in Latin translates to "sleepy transformation," the species that flies the farthest—three thousand miles from the boreal forests in Canada to the oyamel-fir trees in Mexico—on wings spanning a mere four inches. I know that the monarchs fly in what amounts to a cloud, their orange-white-and-black wings stained glass in motion, and I know that their flight is meant to be uninterrupted. So I stood there, awash in sorrow, as I imagined them falling, one by one from the sky. It's a sacred thing to come upon a trace of the fallen, to witness the wings fading before your eyes, to witness how fragile all of this is, to be brushed by the mystery and all of the fluttering wonder.

If I'd come upon such a scene in a book I was reading, how the beach had become a burial plot for tissue-thin wings dropped from the night, I would have grabbed a fat yellow highlighter. Or filled up the margin with scribbles and stars. But in the Book of Nature, I don't muddy the page in marginalia (though I might rush home to jot a note in my journals). Rather, I memorize every last breath of it—every shade and sound and sense of it—and I tuck it away where I'll never forget.

There's no other reading that's like it. I mean, I've had plenty of times of sitting in pews in churches or synagogues, when I've just heard a line from whoever's preaching and I'm stirred to reach for my backpack in search of a pen—before I forget what so moved me. But the impact, sitting on a hard wooden pew, hearing words that all but evaporate before they've crossed the nave, it's nothing like the shoulder-seizing attention that stops you there at the water's edge—your toes tickled by sand, waves gurgling and whooshing, the glint of the sunlight sending up sparks—as you take in what's left of the night-passing monarchs, who year after year turn the sky to a cloud of fluttering flame. All these years later, indelibly inked.

When you're making a habit of seeing this way, as if each page is seen through a sacred transparency, you begin to ask questions beyond the obvious, to ferret out wisdom or truth, to come to know something more of the God who imagined the butterfly, or the one now attuned to not walking by, upkicking sand onto beauty's last gasp.

The water's edge is a church without walls, where the sky is the dome and the vault is forever; its very architecture demands the propelling of thoughts, the launching of bottomless prayer into the heavens.

We've been drawn there since the dawn of all civilization. The great waterways trace through history, blue veins of lifeblood, drawing a thirsty people. It's a geography learned in most every middle school: the Tigris and Euphrates; the Nile, believed to be the causeway between life and death, paired with its celestial mirror in the night sky, the cluster of stars we know as the Milky Way, the Nile in the Sky to the ancient Egyptians. In China, civilization rose along the banks of the Yangtze and the Yellow rivers, and here in the heartland, we've got the muddy Mississippi rolling from the Land of Ten Thousand Lakes, past cornfields and cotton fields, down toward the Delta, where it spills into the Gulf, and on toward the oceans that ever churn.

We are a sea-seeking people; we see something in it, something deep and far beyond words. "In water that departs forever and forever returns, we experience eternity," wrote Mary Oliver, whose daily muse was the Atlantic tide as it washed over and over the Cape Cod coastline. The medieval mystic Mechtild of Magdeburg, a German city on the Elbe River, was moved less by the crashing waves of the sea than by its rippling tide, which as she saw it was a rippling tide of love, one that "flows secretly out from God into the soul and draws it mightily back into its Source."

From my prayer place, bowed beneath the tabernacular sky, in the filtered sunlight of any old morning, or keeping watch as the just-born stars turn on in the twilight, it is the stillness I seek, the stillness that settles me. And the pull of the unalterable tide that draws out my soul's boundless whispers.

I have come to the place where the prayer comes. And so, too, comes the One who utters in wordless reply.

EARTH'S
TURNING

Ecclesiastes was onto something. While an exuberant ephemerality is at the heart of the ancient book, its boiled-down truth is one we hum in our heads for good reason: for everything there is a season, a time for every matter under heaven. And, if pressed to point to proof of the sheer genius at work in the cogs and the gears of creation, the faithful wheeling of the year would be my number one exhibit: the undulations of earth's turning, the rhythms of shadow and light, heat and cold, the enlivening and the dying and all the tug and the pull and the paradox in between, that brings us the carousel of ever-shifting season.

More than anything it teaches me trust, with a chaser of awe.

The way we're nearly at wit's end, can't take one more day of the gloom or the cold or the inferno, and then suddenly it starts to give way, a softening comes, the heavens shift, and we're on to the next picture show. How there's a soulful omniscience ever on watch and at work—a hop, skip, and a jump ahead of little old worrying, wearying us. Rebirth is its constant; no wonder we're brought to our knees.

Each season, in four quarter turns, brings forth its own headlines. There's the yin and yang of spring, the season of exodus and resurrection, of equal parts heartbreak and magic. "The fizz and the roar of the land coming back to life again," is how Robert Macfarlane brilliantly captured the vernal animations. There's summer with its invitation for indolence, for taking it slow, savoring, all but licking your plate of its succulence. And autumn, the season that changes its tense, is letting-go time, the beginning of burrowing in, when the shadow grows longer and sunlight goes amber, when half the globe is stripping to its essence, revealing its unadorned spines. Then there's winter, the stillest of all, when deep-down stirrings are all but invisible, and we learn to keep faith. Sometimes I think God couldn't decide which channel was best, so the heavens kept jabbing the clicker.

It's a wonder reel that never ends, yet never truly repeats—a koan for the ages.

I often contemplate the geometries of time, how the year is not an inescapable circle, a shape that would get us nowhere, but rather it's a spiral, and from one winter to the next we're never the same, always ascending, closer to the holiness we were meant to be—or so that's the hope and the plan, anyway. Maybe that's why God keeps this seasonal show on autoplay: maybe God knows how dense we are in the figuring-it-out department, how some of the lessons we need to review. Over and over and over again. Most especially at the fraying hems of the seasons when the doubt begins to creep in, the fear that we'll never be loosed from whatever it is that tangles and knots us, and God needs to show us those few immutable threads: Resurrection comes. Quiet must follow exuberance. So too dormancy. Surrender to earth's holy rhythms, the very ones that pull the tides and the flocks, paint the woods, star-stitch the night sky. Expect heartbreak. Await healing. Start all over again.

"The seasons are our scripture text," writes Celtic spiritualist Christine Valters Paintner. "This earth we are riding keeps trying to tell us something with its continuous scripture of leaves," echoes William Stafford, a poet and pacifist who referred to himself as "one of the quiet of the land." To the ancient Celts, the unfolding of the seasons read as "gospel without haste." And Walt Whitman, America's latter-day Homer, put something of a military spin to it when he wrote that "nature marches in procession, in sections, like the corps of an army."

What they're all saying, it seems, is that the sweep itself is where the whole sum lies, though each part is its own bottomless cache of wonder—sensory, yes, but spiritual, too. While we might find ourselves immersed in every quarter turn of the year, there is wisdom in stepping back from it, tracing the way one unfolds into the next. That's where prologue and epilogue bookend the hearts of the matter, where we begin to build a sense of deep and abiding faith; the afterword will come, whatever is the thing we long for. It's the eternal promise, one that God wrote into the script from the very genesis. Quite literally, when in the Book of Genesis, it's spelled out in what amounts to God's all-time guarantee: "As long as the earth endures, seedtime and harvest, cold and heat, summer and winter, day and night, shall not cease" (Gen 8:22). It's perpetual, a never-endingness that for some of us might be hard to sink our certainties into, were it not played on rewind.

One of its quieter, more resonant beauties, perhaps, is the way this turning again and again brings us a chronology counted out in the rustlings and the returns of heaven and earth: the return of the Siberian squill in the springtime, that tender tiny cobalt-blue flag that carpets the woodlands come April; the return of the chevron of geese streaking September's clotted-cloud sky; the return of thickening birdsong as early as the dregs of late February, when we're certain the snows will never dwindle, and the world will ever be gray. With each coming again, that deep-down tucked-away place in our memory is tickled, the place that asks, and remembers, *Where was I the last time—the last time I clutched tender stems of Siberian squill in my fist; the last time the goose's cry shook me from my stupors; the last time the birdsong offered its promise? And the time before that? And the very first time? And as very far back as I can possibly think?* It's the marking of time in the embroideries of God's voluptuous making. And it makes for an existence layered and layered in the intricate spirals that twist and turn and come round again, echoing the blessedness and the brokenness and all the growing betwixt and between. It's God's gentle way of inviting soulful inventory by way of the pages that turn in our very own blessed Book of Creation.

For me, it's lily-of-the-valley, that nodding springtime tendril that rises up in the old sod of old woodlands. I can't see it without remembering what might be my lifetime's first instance of awe, unbridled. I remember only these things: my papa, a man I adored beyond words, was at the wheel of his circa-1960 turquoise Ford Falcon, and he'd pulled off the road at the edge of a woods. I, a wee thing of three, maybe four, was wearing my party shoes, not the red Keds I usually wore to the woods but my black patent leathers with the pearly button at the end of the strap. I remember stepping out of the car, and planting my party shoe gingerly onto the leaf-carpeted earth. I know I stepped carefully because I didn't want to crush the perfect little bells that dangled from stalks all around. And then I remember the moment I'll never forget: looking up from my shoe and beyond all the trees, all I saw was an ocean of snow-white bells, nodding and bobbing and perfuming the woods with the purest essence of springtime. I've always wondered if that's how heaven would feel, should I get there some day. But what I *know* is that's my template for awe, a sensory remembering so very strong that, to this day, on the very first day in springtime when I spy my first lily-of-the-most-blessed-valley, I find myself considering awe, asking myself if I've submitted myself to its powers of late. And if the answer is no, I know I need to get to work. To pay closer attention. To put myself in awe's way.

It's symphonic beyond measure, the way the seasonal threads are woven, how one gives in to another, how each holds up another. How the fallow seasons of autumn and winter are when the fields soak in the groundwork they'll need to spring forth come sowing time. How the seed-studded cones of the pine in autumn will fall to the ground, give rise to the summer's sequoia or cedar, how some of those cones hold the seeds for a thousand summers. Or, within a single season, how heaven and earth intermingle, the way springtime's lightning strikes release from the air the nitrogen the seedlings need to surge skyward. Or, consider the cottonwood tree and its summer dance with the sunlight: when the leaves flutter in the wind, sunlight finds its way in, to be filtered through the whole tree. The motion in the upper branches gives the tippy-top leaves a break from the full-strength solar burn, and opens channels for a flickering supply of necessary photons (essential to the chlorophyll equation that makes for green summer garb) to drift to the lower-down leaves. The whole cottonwood thus absorbs what it needs to carry on its earth-saving respirations: breathing in carbon dioxide, exhaling oxygen, all with assist from the light of the sun and the flurry of leaves that clap in the wind. Who imagines such exquisite intricacies? Such gobsmacking invention?

Let me point out a curious thing about this reading of the Book of Nature. That cartwheel of questions and curiosities—probing and pondering the inner workings of one species of trees—is not one into which I'd fling myself if left to my own truth-seeking adventures. I assure you I could sit under a cottonwood for the next two moons and never once contemplate its sunscreening capacities. I'm not equipped in any which way to look at a leaf or a limb or even a trunk and consider arboreal engineering. A necessary appendage for all my earthly and celestial inquisitions is my coterie of literary companions, the trail guides and seers I park on my bookshelves. My shelves are stuffed with all of natural science—astronomy to zoology, with ample spaces reserved for birds, bumblebees, and every which bramble. David George Haskell, a mind-blowing biologist who romps the surrounds of Sewanee, Tennessee's Smoky Mountains, is my eyes and my ears of the woods and the trees and the birds that hover therein. His illuminations carry me far beyond my own natural borders. (*And* he's the one who taught me a thing or three about the cottonwood and its sun dance.)

Back in the Middle Ages, when the theological construct of the Book of Nature was first emerging, it wasn't long till scholars began to insist the Book of Nature was to be read in tandem with Scripture, the Holy Book of the Word. The seventeenth-century British polymath Sir Thomas Browne once wrote, "There are two books from whence I collect my divinity." And while that's a perfectly wise way to read, I prefer to amend the construct. I too believe in reading in tandem, but I say don't stop at the Bible. There are bookshelves galore to be mined. I'd miss five-sixths of the wonder if not for the knowledge I glean from a whole host of texts. I read poets. I read naturalists. I read saints and long-ago mystics. I read and I read and I read. My reading opens exponentially my eyes and my imagination.

I needn't lace up my mukluks to be toppled by natural wonder. I can be equally awestruck curled in my armchair turning page after page, or sprawled in my reading nook, the one that looks into gnarled branches of locust and serviceberry, where sparrows get tipsy on autumn's boozy pluckings. In my insatiable quest to never let up on my collecting of wonder, I've come to think of my literary intake as the Russian-doll rabbit-hole school of reading. One title leads to the next, and I follow the trail of esoterica as deep as it goes. Or until the starlight signals it's well past my bedtime. In my book, the Book of Nature belongs in a paired reading approach more aptly titled the Two-Thousand Book Theology.

It's transfixing, the whole of it. No wonder poets and painters, all those who keep close watch, are drawn to its boundless variations, each a study of creation in motion, ever new, often timeless. Always, always, wholly holy. "Creation is here and now," wrote Henry Beston, the naturalist and Yankee poet, in a letter to an old friend, quoting his own last chapter of *Outermost House*. "We are not living on a mechanism running down like a clock but on an earth sustained by an ever-creating, outpouring stream of the divine imagination."

Here, a few of the seasonal scribblings I've winnowed from each quarter turn of that divine imagining, poured out in a reel without end:

For starters, take springtime, season of quickening, season of equal parts shadow and light—the very equation at its astronomical heart, the vernal equinox marking the fleeting moment when earth's axis aligns directly with the sun, and the planet is neatly halved with equal allotments of light, and the sun shines squarely on the equator. Emily Dickinson calls springtime "a sacrament," and as always she nails it, certainly when you consider the dictionary definition of sacrament as "a means of divine grace." Hard to think otherwise of the "trumpet call of the return of light," as Beston saw it, or "the unsealing of the waters of earth," come the warming-up months in winter's wake. "The earth everywhere, like something talking to itself, murmured and even sang with its living waters and its living streams." I think of those stirrings from deep underground as part of the ablutions of springtime, the rinse of the in-rushing air when the staleness of winter is broomed out the door. When at last we can kick off our snow boots and dare to bare flesh, goosebumps be darned. Springtime, when one minute the tenderlings are breaking through the earth's thawing crust and then—kebang!—the snows fall, is the season for teaching resilience. It's with pang in the heart that we tiptoe out in the dawn, to dust the ice cakes and crystals off the furled petals of snowdrop and earliest daffodil. And how can our souls not feel resuscitated when at daybreak the birdsong is limitless and cadenzas are flung from the boughs? But, just as certainly, April's tempestuous winds will topple the robin's nest from the nook where it was wedged. To come upon a fallen mud-daubed construction, one now cradling orbs broken open, is to be pierced by the merciless pangs of the season of starting over again, with death an inevitable and unavoidable shard at the root of that proposition.

Come summer, the *que-sera* season, when we slow to an indolent saunter, master the art of doing little to nil, we've all the time in the world to indulge in the plenitudes: bare toes in the grass, sweet pea from the pod on the vine, long lazy eves under the stars. It's when daylight is at its longest, as the sun travels its longest, northernmost arc, and night is clipped at both ends. Summertime is when the lightning bug blinks, and the opera of dusk—katydid, cicada, and cricket—chirrs till the last of the stars blink on, and the blazing sun "thickens the air to jelly," so says Annie Dillard, polestar of paying seasonal attention. It's when I might take in a lesson from that master of unbridled zest, the bumblebee, who skitters from one pollen-painted pin cushion to another, her flight path a zig and a zag. She is basically flying in circles, delectable circles, filling her belly with the gold dust of summer's unquenchable thirst. The wide-bellied bee offers this wise instruction: hesitate not, the hour is now, the high tide of summer won't wait. Summertime, you might say, is when God indulges, too, in God's green period, for instance; the bold exhibitionist strutting the stuff of an infinite paint set. "Everything has its own green: cattails, willow leaves, the flip side of an aspen leaf, the gray-green sage, the yellow-green native pasture, the loden timber," writes James Galvin in *The Meadow*, his hundred-year history of a meadow on the Colorado-Wyoming border, a work that's part novel, part natural history. It's "as if the meadow were a green ear held up to listen to the sky's blue." On the subject of God's many greens, there is Rabbi Nachman of Breslav, the late-eighteenth-century sage, who enthused, "How good it is to pray to God and meditate in the meadows amidst the grass and the trees. When one goes out to the meadows to pray, every blade of grass, every plant and flower enter his prayers and help him, putting strength and force into his words." The wise rabbi urged the prayerful to find pastureland: "Go to a grassy field, for the grass will awaken your heart." Indeed, the profusions of summertime seem meant to immerse us in the surround sound of uncorkable wonder.

And then comes the season of awe, the molasses-lit days of autumn, the liminal season, one that cultural critic Maria Popova claims is "by far the most paradoxical," wedged between equinox and solstice. "It moors us," she writes, "to cosmic rhythms of deep time and at the same time envelops us in the palpable immediacy of its warm afternoon breeze, its evening chill, its unmistakable scentscape." It begins at the appointed hour, the hour of equinox, when the sun slides into absolute right angle to earth, its beams falling straight onto the equator, not angled either which way, north or south, and, once again, it's equal light for all. Until the morrow, when the northern shadow lengthens and we're spinning toward winter. Before the winter in all its nakedness comes, the days of autumn go up in glory, a blaze of fiery-tinged woodland and meadow, when the north wind "sweetens the persimmons and numbs the last of the crickets and hornets," when it "fans the flames of the forest maples, bows the meadow's seeded grasses, and pokes its chilling fingers under the leaf litter." So wrote Dillard, from her post in the Roanoke Valley. It's the evanescence of autumn that underscores its beauties, amplifies the seasonal truth to behold what's before you now, for it won't be for long. Pico Iyer, the British-born writer who spent much of his life in a Benedictine monastery in Big Sur, California, and now spends a good chunk of the year in suburban Japan, writes in *Autumn Light: Season of Fire and Farewell*, "We cherish things, Japan has always known, precisely because they cannot last; it's their frailty that adds sweetness to their beauty. In the central literary text of the land, *The Tale of Genji*, the word for 'impermanence' is used more than a thousand times." Autumn, he writes, "poses the question we all have to live with: How to hold on to the things we love even though we know that we and they are dying. How to see the world as it is, yet find light within that truth."

Which brings us to the year's season of ending *and* beginning: winter, in all its divinities of beauty, begins in the deep darkness of the longest night, and from there on out the whole stretch is marching toward the light, minute by minute brightening at either edge of the night's inky slumber. Winter's curtain rises at the precise moment the north pole is tilted farthest from the sun, and the shadow cast across the northerly globe is at its longest. The celestial concordance of shadow and light draws all creation inward: bears crawl into caves, painted turtles bury themselves in the pond bottom and take not a breath the whole winter long, honeybees deep in the hive shiver en bloc to keep from freezing. We, too, put a human spin to our hibernations: logs to the fire, toes under blankets, arms through the sleeves of thick woolen sweaters. Against the darkness, winter skies shine brighter than ever, with more double and triple stars than any season of the year, and Orion, the great hunter, vaults with his bow and his hounds across the heavenly dome. The long night, dappled with starlight, draws our wonder. It's the season of stillness, all around. It's the season of Advent, of awaiting, anticipating, the newborn wonder. It's the season of starting over, beginning again, etching new promises, launching new prayer. And often, especially here in the middlelands, not far from where Arctic winds whip down the neck of the lake, with snowfalls measured in feet not inches, when polar vortex is encoded in the winter's vernacular, it's the time of extremes, when all of creation is pushed to its limits. And that's why I keep close watch in winter on its permeabilities, when the cell wall between the wild and the worldly is punctured, when the precious little wild things—be they feathered or furry—come out into the open, all but tap on the windowpane, emerging from their secret hiding grounds in search of necessary sustenance. The birds seek seed, the bushy-tailed ones take whatever I toss their way. Each morning, no matter what the heavens are hurling my direction, I don my make-believe farmer-girl boots, grab my battered old tin, and head out for what you might call *matins*, morning's benediction from the book of uncommon prayer. I bow to the heavens, unfurl a few vespers, fill my feeders with seed. It's in this fragile interplay, between the wild things and me, when we reach beyond what we know, extend an open palm of pure unbridled trust, that I find myself in the very act of holy veneration. I come bearing sustenance, in the form of plain seed. And I'm awash in the knowing that the wilds have wisdoms to teach, should we surrender to them, leave behind our worldly know-it-all-ness, and expose ourselves to their murmurings and their whispers. Mercy is among its urgencies. Mercy is what we need to remember, deep in the stronghold of winter. Who ever thought to bring such wonder to winter? The wild begs questions that only the heavens can answer for me.

And so the year, in all its seasons, is a never-ending book of intelligence, divine intelligence, ever ancient and new. It is in these topographies of time, the geographies of wonder, the ones that come as we're walking the year, that we stand our one best chance for intimate encounter with the Almighty, the Cloudmaker, the Heavens Opener, the Star-Kindler, the Leaf-Cutter, the One Who Puts Flight to the Wing. I think of the words of Meister Eckhart: "God's ground is my ground and my ground is God's ground." And so, too, time; be it taken in chapter or stanza—summer or autumn, winter or spring— or in the whole volume's unspooling as inscribed in Ecclesiastes: a time to be born, a time to die; a time to plant, and a time to pluck up what is planted. A time to behold, a time for every blessing under heaven.

A LITANY OF
ASTONISHMENTS

Let me keep company always with those who say
  "Look!" and laugh in astonishment,
  and bow their heads.

— Mary Oliver, Pulitzer Prize–winning American poet

❧ When a bear is sick it wanders mountainsides and fields searching for herbs, grasses, leaves, and flowers that hold the power of healing. One such balm in the ursine apothecary is a root found in the western Rockies, known by the Aztecs as *chuchupate*, their ancient name for "bear medicine." It's also called oshá, bear root, or lovage (*Ligusticum porteri*). Bears, who happen to be the herbalists of the animal kingdom (they make use of more than forty species of plants), seek out the oshá roots in the spring, just as they're lumbering around in the wake of their long winter's nap. Once they sniff it out, the bears dig madly, rubbing oshá—an excretory stimulant—all over themselves. Makes sense that after a long, deep sleep, the hibernators would seek to get things flowing again (from lungs, kidneys, intestines, and skin). But those wily bears don't stop at the medicine chest: male bears are known to use oshá in romance, presenting the knobby root to the female of their pursuit during vernal courtship.

❧ The spider's web is an intricate piece of precision engineering. Made from large proteins, it's sticky, stretchy, and tough. So it's no surprise that many small birds—including one little wonder named the Anna's hummingbird—make a point of collecting strands of spider silk to use in nest construction. Spider silk not only acts as a glue, holding the nest together, but it's flexible enough to accommodate the growing bodies of nestlings.

ᥫ Monarchs, the one of all twenty-four thousand species of butterflies that migrates the farthest—upward of three thousand miles, on a flight of two months, the most evolutionarily advanced migration of any known butterfly, perhaps any insect—come back, each year, to the very same ancestral tree, the very one of their own earlier generations. Talk about a family tree.

ᥫ Here's another fine thing: monarchs drink from the mist and the fog. They drink while they're flying and when they land in the fall—in oyamel-fir trees down in Mexico if they're monarchs from east of the Rockies, or in eucalyptus coves along California's Pacific Coast if they're from west of the Rockies—they quench their thirst, a considerable thirst, you might well imagine, from the ocean mist that rolls into the coves, and the fog clouds that settle high in the Mexican mountains.

ᥫ Most of the year, the monarch lives an ephemeral life. Within weeks, it dies. Not so autumn's monarchs, the Methuselah generation—named for the Bible's oldest man, who lived "nine hundred sixty-nine years" (Gen 5:27). Monarchs born at summer's end live eight months. They exist for one purpose: to fly south, and come spring, beget the next generation. Who in heaven's name dreamed up such almighty wonder?

THE LIMINAL

BIRDS

I couldn't tell you how old I was the first time I tended a bird in a box. The edge of the frame is hazy, but I do know this: there was a box, a shoebox, maybe a grocery store box, and it would have been left overnight tucked against the house, or maybe moved into the garage. I would run from my bed, before I'd even rubbed the sleep from my eyes. And, heart pounding (my own), I would kneel, the veneration pose, and peek over the edge. There would be my feathered little friend, my rescue from the wilds, quivering in the corner, my Kleenex night cover tossed off to the side. I would begin my ministrations, sometimes with droplets of water, sometimes with morsel of worm. Always with a certain belief that if that bird was to live through the night, if I was to find its feathery chest pulsing with heartbeat come morning, it needed my unbroken attention. There is a long catena of birds in my boxes in my lifetime. Broken-winged birds. Birds who'd banged into windows. Birds who'd tumbled from boughs. In the house where I grew up, a downed bird was a thing of alarm. And in its woundedness, in the hours-long devotion that sometimes stretched into days, I would learn that every once in a while a veil would be lifted, and our holy task was to reach across with our own open palm, to entwine with the wild, to enter the realm of unbridled creation. Even if only for infirmary purposes.

I learned early of a sacred entwinement, realized that even in our word-lessness, simple gestures of kindness—between creature and child, creature and whomever takes care—might open us up to reciprocities and little-read epistles of wonder and awe. The curtains between us are porous. And my enchantments with birds are many, a nesting doll of enchantments, one inside another and another, always another. It all began when I held in my hand a fluffball of feathers and wee scratchy feet, a sum of creation that weighed in at no more than the fractions of gram that equal three aspirin.

I came by my avian affections ancestrally. My grandmother, a woman whose ample bosom belied any particular softness, had one striking exception to her often tough disposition: she doted on birds. Specifically, owls, wrens, and chickadees. She'd slide open her grand dining room window and scatter toast crumbs or spoonfuls of seed and suet onto the little perch she'd attached to the sill. I watched closely these fenestral ministrations, mesmerized by her cooing, and the tender care she displayed. Once, I was told, she opened her palm and a chickadee landed.

My mother, too, has long read the skies as if scanning for signs from the heavens. In the months after my father died, too young, my mother, a widow at fifty, would report the low sweep of a hawk, the way it circled overhead, or landed on a branch and would not budge, as if a message from beyond that we were to read as *All is well here; please carry on.* While the reportage might have rubbed me as naive, as something close to too wishful, I reconsidered when it happened to me. The rare few times an unseen bird—a Cooper's hawk, a great horned owl—has rustled branches, stirred the air, uttered creaturely cries amid my proximities, I too have stood rapt. I, too, have felt the otherworldly. And wondered.

There is mystery aplenty in the realm of the birds. Where do they sleep at night? Where do they hide from the cold? How is it that they teach their young to sing? How, oh how, do they crisscross the globe, coming back to roost in the same thicket of alder or birch, on the same savannah, the same side of the mountain? The unanswerability of these queries—unanswerable at least for a nonornithologist like me—reminds me that even though I have no clue where the robin sleeps at night, or how the cardinal stays alive in the polar vortex, there are answers, beyond my knowing. And in that same vein it's not too much of a leap to remind me that the mysteries of God, the unanswerability of godly form and ways, do not mean there are no answers. I learn in my ignorance to be comfortable, to become acquainted with the terra incognita that interrupts the map of my consciousness.

I grew up with my eyes on the sky. I knew the red cardinal from the scarlet tanager nearly as early as I knew A from E. What stirs me now is the way the red bird scythes through the otherwise two-toned tableau of winter's drab. How the shock of crimson wing can stir me. Like monastery bells calling postulants to prayer, the sudden swoop of cardinal is as if a tap to the heart, a solemn bow of the head, a bending of the knees, a short sweet inkling that God is near. It's the eruption of red on the washed-out tableau that ignites in me a call to attention, and marveling soon opens into quiet whispered prayer. As Meister Eckhart once wrote, "If the only prayer you ever say in your life is thank you, it will be enough." When the cardinal plants his plump red self on the ledge just beyond my window, I can't help but whisper *thank you, thank you, thank you.*

I count the blessing of the birds as if beads slipped on a prayer cord.

For starters, theirs is the realm between heaven and earth. They carry the sky on their backs, is how Thoreau put it. They're a piece of the sky, is what Mary Oliver thought. We see it day after day, hour upon hour, whether we press our nose to the window, or watch from below heaven's dome: there they are with their figure eights in the sky, the parabolas of flight, sometimes etched like checkmarks against the clouds. They swoop and they dart, they claim the tops of the trees. As long as humans have been inscribing or telling our stories, the birds—almost oracular, often with mystery, messengers of the gods—have held our attentions. And our divinations. Muhammad saw the spread wings of birds as prayer, giving praise to Allah, each one, according to the Qur'an, "knowing its own mode of prayer." Birdsong was considered a secret and perfect language, "the language of angels," in Sufi wisdom. Jesus preached of God's compassion for sparrows, and likened himself to a hen tucking her chicks under her wings.

It's not hard to hear birdsong and imagine holy melody. The dawn chorister at my house just happens to be the scarlet-robed cardinal. And whenever I'm witness to that first bright note breaking the silence, I can only hear it as lauds, praise be to the God of the rising sun. All through the day, waxing and waning, the song threads through the air. At night, too: Roger Deakin, the late British stalker of the wilds, told a charming story of rooks chorusing outside an English village, and a little girl going to bed remarking that the birds "were saying their prayers."

It's all an acoustic marvel, one beyond the wildest invention.

Pablo Neruda once asked,

how
out of its throat
smaller than a finger
can there fall the waters
of its song?

Turns out there's a bird part the size of a pea or a lentil, called the syrinx (named after the nymph turned into a reed by Pan, the ancient Greek god of fields, flock, and fertility). It lies deep in the chest of the bird, a delicate structure with two tissue-thin membranes, a dozen ringed bones, and two dozen muscles among the fastest known, capable of contracting two hundred times per second. As the air flows out from the bird's lungs, the membranes tremble, the sound almost "sculpted," on a millisecond timescale, as many as thirty-six notes per second, in the case of the winter wren.

"Birds are quick-fingered jewelers of air," writes biologist David George Haskell, "crafting dozens of ornamented gems every second." Close to half of the birds on the planet are songbirds, some four thousand species, which means through and across every forest and plain and savannah, deep in the jungle and high in the mountains, the air is bristling with hoots and yodels and caws, the byzantine song of a sedge warbler, or the seamless duets of a pair of plain-tailed wrens. Baby birds begin their singing lessons while still under wraps, inside the unhatched egg, where they listen attentively to the bird who amounts to their tutor, usually the papa bird, surprisingly. It takes but sixty-five days for the little birds to work their way through the song book, from quavering first notes, to something more recognizable, on its way to crystallized song, each ancestral tune passed through the generations. Scientists tell us that fledglings will toss out some one to two million syllables of trial and error on their way to treetop aria. Truth be told, it's all love song, powered by lust. And no one bests the male house wren seeking a mate, a champion yodeler belting out as many as six hundred songs in an hour. It all sounds like praise song to me.

But what of those other ornithological marvels: the birds' knack for constructing their nurseries, twig by twig, blade by blade of dried grass, often upholstered with tuft of dandelion fluff. And without so much as a single hour of sit-down instruction. Or, the twice-yearly pilgrimage that is migration, riding the currents, charting the stars, crossing the globe, drawn by insatiable pull toward feeding or breeding grounds, all in pursuit of extending the species. There are birds, mind you, who flap featherweight wings for thousands of miles—not a pause for water or food—and come back to the very same nest, one that's been theirs for countless generations. If God gave us these marvels, these singers of song and riders of wind, surely they're here to impart some holy wisdom. If only we look and we listen.

Consider the nest: No less than the great architect Ludwig Mies van der Rohe once extolled the wonders of the grass-and-leaf-and-twig constructions of birds, and remarked, "They echo like old songs." Terry Tempest Williams, examining a swallow's nest, declared it "natural history unfolding." Birds, the original tailors, are known to sew, weave, or bind their nests. Ingenious at the art of bricolage, remaking found bits into something altogether new, their materials are numberless: spider webs bind the nest of the eastern wood peewee; the ruby-throated hummingbird builds a nest no bigger than a walnut, lines it with thistledown or cattail, and hides it under lichens; the apostlebird molds a clay pot of a nest, daubing mud to a thickness of seven inches. It's a process triggered by sunlight, which surges hormones in both the mama and papa birds as the hours of daylight intensify and grow longer. The choreographies of the cosmos—nest-building season coinciding with fruit-bearing season on trees, a built-in bodega for mama bird—astound. It takes but three to four days for a simple nest construction, and up to twenty for the most elaborate. It's all primal, the unswerving pursuit toward dodging extinction.

And it abounds with accommodations, determined to beat formidable odds. Egyptian plovers are known to bury their eggs in the sand on days when it's especially hot, and to dribble cool water from nearby shallows should temperatures soar. A black-capped chickadee might remodel a woodpecker's left-behind hole, or pound out its own in the rotten stump of a tree. Because the nesting stage is when baby birds are most vulnerable, a main defense is camouflage. But that's not the only precaution. European starlings, avian herbalists, weave wild carrot or yarrow into their nests to keep out pesky little mites. The intricacies of the hatchery, once those eggs are laid, boggle the mind. Even the science of the egg alone is magical—dare I say divine. At once porous enough for oxygen to flow through, the shells are precisely strong enough to bear the weight of the mama bird. The feel of the eggs pressing against her breast stimulates the production of a hormone that furthers incubation and then, in doves and pigeons, stimulates something called "pigeon milk," a white secretion from the glands that will be fed to young squabs. Indeed, once the eggs are hatched, the birds' sole focus is feeding. Phoebes, a plump songbird, forage as many as 1,700 trips per pair in a twelve-hour period. Hellbent on survival of the species, birds will, sadly, waste no energy on the feeble. If food is scarce, the mama and papa will give the least food to the baby bird with the palest mouth lining, as that's a telltale indication of a weak little nestling. In most small perching birds, the time from fresh egg to flight may be an action-packed twenty days, in which that fledgling will have absorbed an entire syllabus, from how to sing to how to navigate the night sky.

It dizzies me, the whole unimaginable script of it. Even from my periphery, merely reading from here on the sidelines, straining to imbibe even a gulp from this firehose of unfathomability, I stand in awe. It's as close as I edge to staking my flag in the certainty that none of this comes by accident or happenstance. Science just might explain it away, but in my book this is where I fling myself—knowingly, willingly—into the deep end of faith. I'll take a God of infinite wonder every last time.

Now, ponder migration: navigating by stars, magnetic fields, and polarized light, with no other guidance than some urge deep in their chromosomes—ancestral memory, the instinct for pilgrimage—birds follow the ancient call to be fruitful and multiply, "obeying impulses beyond our cognition," writes Robert Macfarlane. That these delicate birds, by the tens of millions, take to the skies come the shifting of light in the fall and the spring, undertaking epic journeys across continent, equator, and hemisphere, defies belief, writes natural historian Scott Weidensaul, author of *Living on the Wind*, an exploration of the avian phenomenon that stitches continents via airborne invisible thread. Since the fifteenth century, when sailors first noted the migrations of songbirds and shore birds, "orientation research," the broad field of migration studies, has fine-tuned the lenses of ornithologists and poets. And the occasional theologian as well. The Old Testament, in fact, makes migrational notice of the stork and the turtle dove, the crane and the swallow, "observing the time of their coming."

All these millennia later, it's now known that come fall, when the Northern Hemisphere shadows grow longer and the daylight thins, there will come a clear night with a brisk northerly tailwind when millions of songbirds will vault into the skies, flapping wings twenty times per second, for forty to fifty hours at altitudes of five thousand feet, showing up on radar "like ghosts beneath the moon," or hieroglyphs against the clouds, streaming toward ancestral grounds, often a continent away. On one exceptional autumn night off Cape Cod some years back, radar showed some twelve million songbirds passed overhead. The sky on those nights—be it autumn or spring—is thick with the flapping of wings "as fragile as a whisper," Weidensaul writes. In all, more than five billion birds annually weave this migrational tapestry. And not only is the night alive with unseen stirrings, it's alive with "secret sounds, monosyllabic flight calls, lovely in their simplicity, like Shaker hymns." The ancients, long keyed in to the murmurings of the cosmos, referred to this as "the music of the spheres." And for most species, it's a leap of blind faith, led purely by instinct, with nary a tour guide. For the bristle-thighed curlew, for example, only five weeks out of the egg, its parents long gone from its marshy homeland, the diminishing daylight flicks a neurohormonal switch and a restlessness that prompts test flights and premigratory drills before suddenly—with no adults to lead the way—the little birds take flight. The great restlessness, which all but shakes the sky, is labeled *Zugunruhe* (*Zug*,

German for "move," and *unruhe* for "restless" or "anxiety"), a term coined by the German ornithologist who proved birds were using a sophisticated solar compass, though it was later found that the sun is only part of the equation. The scientific flocks who study these things figured out that birds take their cues, too, from the stars, and the sounds of this rumbling earth. Wind, ocean surf, earthquake tremor, volcanic eruption, thunderstorms as far as five hundred miles away, all feed into the navigational soundtrack, so the night fliers, southbound or northbound, bend with the curve of whatever the globe hurls their way. I shudder to think how we earth-bound humans, plodding along with our numbing dependencies on GPS, could barely make it nowadays from one side of town to another if left to our own sorry devices. Our wayfinding ways, at risk of extinction.

In short, all of this science leaves me in a state of pure wonder. Maybe, you too. I unspool all of it because too often the flocks are unnoticed, the intricacies unknown. To encounter the full force of the Almighty sometimes you need to look deeper, more closely. The exultation of larks, the parliament of owls, radiance of cardinals, covey of quail (collective names for each of those flocks; in the bird world all have particular names, dreamed up by a long-ago monk, John Lydgate of late-fourteenth-century England), their mysteries and whimsies and marvels hold me rapt. "Let no one think it ridiculous to learn a lesson in virtue from birds," wrote Saint Cuthbert, the early Irish monk, as quoted by the Venerable Bede in the early eighth century.

I think of the last lines in Weidensaul's book on the heavenly flights of the acres of birds, crisscrossing the seas and the continents. On a cold May morning, alongside a stream in the mountains of northern Pennsylvania, the author sat with his eyes closed when a redstart, no bigger than a thumb, let out a warble from a thicket of willow. The little bird prompted these questions, musings from the birdwatcher: "What drives this small creature, barely heavier than air," he wondered. "I can only imagine what has happened to it in its life—what near-brushes with predators it has escaped, what storms have tried to rake it from the sky, what females have taken it as a mate, what dynasties of redstarts it has founded. What thousands of miles have passed beneath its stubby wings."

It's those bigger, deeper questions—taking in the whole sweep of the saga, shifting our lens from up-close to broad view, and back again—that beg to be asked if what we're after is a close read of the great Book of Nature, if what we seek through the lens of our looking glass is something of epiphany. There are so many questions. So much to learn from the improbable flocks.

Against incontrovertible odds—in defiance of gravity, for starters—these wild things take to the winds. "Wildness is a wayward weed," muses ornithologist J. Drew Lanham, professor of wildlife ecology and much-acclaimed author of *The Home Place: Memoirs of a Colored Man's Love Affair with Nature*, and, more recently, *Sparrow Envy*. "But it's also worthy of adoration and worship." He puts a burr to his musings in an essay linking the free flight of wild birds to the enslavement of ancestors seized from west and central Africa. "I wonder about the enslaved watchers who worked in the shadows of endless passenger pigeon flocks that passed overhead, or heard the ivory-bills that called from the tall timber, or glanced the Carolina parakeets that flashed across work-weary eyes." Might they have glanced skyward, imagining themselves unbound by the "weight of oppression," he wonders. "Beyond the monotonous thud slice of a hoe in pluff mud, what would my ancestors have noticed?" Of those flocks passing over sorghum field or salt marsh, where the day-to-day work offered no respite, Lanham writes: "Sweet sounds and beauty are no less worthy of notice because one is in chains—perhaps they are worthier because of the chains."

I don't know that I'll ever again watch an unbound bird tracing ellipses in space, and not think hard about those who cannot break the chains—literal or figurative—that bind them.

Or maybe, more simply, it's what Williams, the poet and naturalist, writes of in *Refuge*, in a chapter titled "Long-Billed Curlew," as she walks a forsaken corner of Utah's salt flats. "I pray to the birds because I believe they will carry the messages of my heart upward. I pray to them because I believe in their existence, the way their songs begin and end each day—the invocations and benedictions of Earth. I pray to the birds because they remind me of what I love rather than what I fear. And at the end of my prayers, they teach me how to listen."

That alone is a plentiful prayer, that we learn how to listen. That enough is a lesson that might take a lifetime.

The great naturalist Aldo Leopold—he of *A Sand County Almanac*, he who'd tramped the marshes awaiting the quail's Ave Maria in the hush of the dawn, who'd planted himself at the top of the hill for no other reason than to watch the geese go by, and who'd called the sandhill crane "the trumpet in the orchestra of evolution"—rarely lifted the veil on his own sense of the sacred. But once, through a story of a boy bedazzled by birds, he wrote of his sacred awakening in the third person. It was a curious grammatical choice, but one for which I am grateful, as I find myself strangely able to read myself in Leopold's "he":

What value has wildlife from the standpoint of morals and religion? I heard of a boy once who was brought up an atheist. He changed his mind when he saw that there were a hundred-odd species of warblers, each bedecked like to the rainbow, and each performing yearly sundry thousands of miles of migration about which scientists wrote wisely but did not understand. No "fortuitous concourse of elements" working blindly through any number of millions of years could quite account for why warblers are so beautiful. No mechanistic theory, even bolstered by mutations, has ever quite answered for the colors of the cerulean warbler, or the vespers of the woodthrush, or the swansong, or—goose music. I dare say this boy's convictions would be harder to shake than those of many inductive theologians. There are yet many boys to be born who, like Isaiah, "may see, and know, and consider, and understand together, that the hand of the Lord hath done this."

In the abyss of the inexplicable, even Leopold turns toward the inexpressible. Might it be that what most startles us toward the sacred is the unanswerability—the impossibly azure warbler, the otherworldly swansong—we confront when gazing at those oracles that soar beneath stars seen or unseen?

Or, maybe it's not so complicated, after all. Maybe all the whisper-winged flocks are asking is that we become part of the silence, make lauds of the dawnsong, and vespers of twilight. Maybe all they're asking is that we behold the way they wheel on the wind, put heartbeat to pilgrimage, dodge what the weather gods hurl. Maybe the quotidian flocks of our own back plots—the little brown birds, and the vibrant-feathered ones who seem to have stepped straight out of the paint set—maybe they're out there squawking and twittering and belting their lungs out in pure invitation: for each of us to reach across, into the fringe of the wild, partake of an unbridled grace. Maybe our simple ministrations, seed in the winter, a spot to wet their whistler come summer, rescue whenever it's called for, maybe that and our willingness to sink into the quiet, maybe that's the whole admission ticket: to feel entwined in the dance of the wild.

Or, maybe, we're meant to plant ourselves under their sky and follow instruction. To pray in an avian way is to mirror the effortlessness of their airborne flight, unbinding our hearts and letting our words spill unstructured, unmeasured, unrhymed; to break into song, spurred by nothing so much as a shift in sunlight or shadow; to sense our own weightlessness in a gravitas world, and allow it to vault us to heights we've not yet considered.

Like the doves who fold their wings over their backs, as hands folded in prayer, we too can learn to cast our own prayer to the upwind and watch its wings row toward the heavens.

GENTLE RAIN, THRASHING STORM

Rain, like most of us, has its moods. In its more laconic hours, it comes on unsuspectingly, without folderol, timpani, or cymbal crashing, the barest slip of a presence and suddenly you're bespattered. On the days when rain is tempestuous, furious, raging, it rattles the heavens, cleaves the night, pummels the trees, and sends all the world—even the puddle-paddling robins—running for cover. Betwixt and between, it's the master of a thousand voices, from the salubrious *plopp*—the drop with a splatter—to the militaristic rat-a-tat-tat, when the rain tries to pretend it's a handful of pebbles thrashing your windows, and on to the audible gulp when a downpour is frothing your gulleys. The Brits, reliably saturated in the subject, offer a lengthy lexicon for precipitation's multiple personalities: there's a basking (drenching in heavy shower); a drisk (misty drizzle); a fox's wedding (sudden drops out of clear blue sky); a hurly-burly (thunder and lightning); a stotting (rain so hard it bounces up off the ground); and, for closers, a thunner-pash (heavy shower with thunder). Because it's so elemental, the life stuff of our very existence, the celestial surge that fills our rivers and waters our crops, rinses away the detritus, bathes all the woods, and the sidewalks as well, it's been the subject of intense preoccupation and prognostication for a long, long time. Since ever ago.

It's "the intake and outbreath of water that's brought the land to life since time immemorial," is how Melissa Harrison captured it in *Rain*, her meditation on the subject, specifically as it falls on England's fens and moors and hedge-rows, something of a sodden epicenter, where Harrison claims the rain is coauthor of the countryside.

Rain manages to stay out of Genesis for six whole chapters, but it makes a thunderous entrance once it pours on Noah's head, and his ark and his zoo besides, carrying on for forty days and nights. It's no wonder the ancient Greeks and Romans pinned galactic powers to the gods of rain and thunder. Pliny, an old Roman, considered lightning the wrath of the sky god, Jupiter (aka Zeus to the Greeks), and the rainbow the varicolored robe worn by the goddess Iris. In the Aztec pantheon of gods, among the most formidable was the old rain god Tlāloc, of whom it was written, "To him was attributed the rain; for he made it, he caused it to come down, he scattered the rain like seed, and also the hail. He caused to sprout, to blossom, to leaf out, to bloom, to ripen, the trees, the plants, our food. And also by him were made floods of water and thunder-bolts." The lesser Aztec rain gods, Tlāloc's sons, were said to keep rain in four jars—one with good rain, one with frost, one with drought, and one with contaminated water. Aztec worshippers did everything under the sun to sway the demigods to crack open, and pour upon the thirsty earth, the jar of good rain.

Rain has a way of catching my attention—and not merely because it pelts at my windowpanes, ranks among heaven's percussives. We pray for it. We sing for it in nursery ditties to go away, come again another day. We dance to bring it on. And we roll out tarps to stop it. The rains that stop me most, the ones that draw me to the window nook, where I keep closest watch, are the ones that come in one of two speeds: gentle lullaby; or thrashing, shake-you-by-the-shoulders, thunder-'n'-lightning exclamation.

To pause to consider the rain is one of the capacities of the soul that might be divinely inspired. Does the otter consider rain? Does the painted turtle? It's one of the exercises in the Book of Nature that swells our soul's capabilities. We need to slow ourselves long enough to allow such questions to bubble to the surface, not unlike the blisters of air that dapple the skim of the pond as the turtle makes its watery way across the mucky bottom.

Reading the Book of Nature, as with any text, can be done in one of two ways: you can skim it, hurriedly turning the pages, on the lookout for high points and plot turns, and you'll walk away with a CliffsNotes sense of it: underwhelmed. Or, you can pore over it, haul out your markers and inks, scribble in margins, enroll in the Rabbit Hole School of reading, where one tome leads to another, and before you know it, you've spent a whole afternoon chasing down threads from one curiosity onto another, in breathless exuberance, enabling you to sit down to dinner and promptly enthrall the whole table (or so you fool yourself) with your endless discoveries of zillions of names for rain in the soggiest places. I am, admittedly, a pupil of the latter.

Long an occupational reader, reviewing books for the soul for the *Chicago Tribune* and its sister papers across the country, I called it my job to cull pages. Along the way, and over the years of wordsmithery, I picked up a habit of squirreling away all the best little bits. Transcribing favorite lines from one's reading is a practice centuries old—commonplacing, it's called: the creation of a commonplace book, a self-inscribed anthology of esoterica and knowledge. In other words, I'm a hoarder of literary persuasion. And I keep noble company: among my brethren, Marcus Aurelius, Thomas Jefferson, Sir Walter Raleigh (while locked in the Tower of London, no less). The Anglo-Irish poet and political satirist Jonathan Swift, in *A Letter of Advice to a Young Poet*, once prescribed the practice thusly:

A common-place book is what a provident poet cannot subsist without, for this proverbial reason, that "great wits have short memories;" and whereas, on the other hand, poets being liars by profession, ought to have good memories. To reconcile these, a book of this sort is in the nature of a supplemental memory; or a record of what occurs remarkable in every day's reading or conversation. There you enter not only your own original thoughts, (which, a hundred to one, are few and insignificant) but such of other men as you think fit to make your own by entering them there.

I've a heavenly friend, a fellow hoarder as it were, who describes her incessant gathering as that of a magpie, feathering her nest with gathered-up swatches of beautiful epiphanic language, in singular words and wisdoms. If, as Mary Oliver insisted, the true work of our lives is our heart's awakening, then this scrupulous business of reading is hardly a dalliance; it is, in fact, imperative spiritual practice.

Which is precisely the reason I've come to read the Book of Nature in a commonplacing sort of a way, hungrily hoarding arcanum and astonishment—from the subtle to the spectacular—as I pore over each of its pages.

Which brings me back to raindrops, always awakening.

In the category "quiet" falls one summer's morning rain when I found myself bent in my garden-troweling pose, rearranging leafy things, and the rain caught me by surprise. It came without throat clearing, no rumble off in the distance. No dark skies foretelling. In fact, the golden orb of sun was shining through the branches of the pine. But there it was, polka-dotting my bare arms. A drop, a plop, another plopp, plopp, plopp, the susurrations of a summer morning's rain. And then a ping hit the blade of my trowel, and it was confirmed: the heavens had sprung the softest, lullingest leak. All at once, I felt my shoulders sigh, and all the rest of me besides. I heard a gentle *whoof* bellow through my lips. The days had been dry, the garden almost crackling. And this unannounced sprinkling felt like all-over answered prayer: for the garden, and for me. I felt, as I plenty often do, as if the long arms of God had all but reached through the clouds, fingers applied to that tight spot just between my eyes, kneading those teeny circles, the kind that make the aches break loose and chase away. All the worries that knotted me, they eased, too. In between the plops, I heard a holy whisper: *be not afraid.* Gentle rain on a summer's morn is something of a wash for the soul, a benediction in drips and drops.

An altogether other brand of rain is the rain that comes combustibly. Those crack-open moments when sunlight's eclipsed, thunder rends the sky, and lightning flashes as if machine-gun fire. God gets our attention, all right.

Leave it to Walt Whitman, the wandering bard, to capture its every drama, as he did in *Specimen Days*, his notes-keeping from the countryside in the wake of the Civil War: "The dark smoke-color'd clouds roll in furious silence athwart the sky; the soft green leaves dangle all around me; the wind steadily keeps up its hoarse, smoothing music over my head—Nature's mighty whisper." And no one beats Henry Beston, listening to the soundtrack of a summer thrasher off the Atlantic, in *Outermost House*: "A thunderstorm is a 'tempest' on the Cape," he writes, using the word as Shakespeare used it, in its old and beautiful Elizabethan meaning of thunder and lightning, literally. "Suddenly the heavens cracked open in an immense instant of pinkish-violet light," filling his windows with "violent, inhuman light." And not long after, as tempers are wont to do, "a tremendous crash then mingled with the withdrawal of the light, and echoes of thunder rumbled away and grew faint in a returning rush of darkness. A moment after, rain began to fall gently as if someone had just released its flow, a blessed sound on a roof of wooden shingles." But then it all rose up again, "flash after stabbing flash amid a roaring of rain, and heavy thunder that rolled on till its last echoes were swallowed up in vast detonations which jarred the walls." The tempests off my Lake Michigan are of barely milder inland vein; I've seen the lightning light up the sky in X-ray inversions, I've seen trees as wide as my waist bend as if at the barre, I've heard the rain on my roof bang out percussions to rival the bucket-drum kids who deafen the crowds on downtown sidewalks.

It's irrefutable that the God of so much subtlety has moments, clearly, of no-holding-back. As it's ever been, this God who thundered to Moses and right through the Psalms, this God who dances in the thunderstorms, as theologian Belden Lane once mused. And what are we to make of a God who plays both ends, and all in between: the God who slips in unawares, soothes us with a summer's lullaby, counted out in raindrops, and then, in a flash, "the One who is the beginning and the end speaks in the mighty reverberations of 'seven thunders,'" as the ancient Celts believed?

"The search is always for the Mystery that is deep within creation and yet infinitely other than anything we can know or name," writes Celtic theologian J. Philip Newell in *The Book of Creation*. That the breadth, from barely audible rainy crepitations to plug-your-ears-and-hide-beneath-the-bedclothes crash-boom-bangings, is so unbridgeable for us ordinary mortals is yet another foothold in our figuring out that this God we seek is indeed immeasurable.

As springtime would have it, I am sitting here now amid a rain that's been at it for days, the ficklest of rains: one minute it's barely pebbling the windows, the next it's making a joke of the downspouts, seeing how hard it can gush. It's even taken a turn as glops of the slushiest semi-snowflakes. It's a rain that can't make up its mind. But whatever its form, it's a rinse. The colorless, still-thawing earth is drinking it up like a runner after a race. I imagine the burgeoning buds whispering *thank you*. And, as with all those weathery interruptions that draw us indoors, it calls to my deep inner monk. It all but insists I take to my nook, press my nose to the panes, keep dedicated vigil. Watching the world turn green is a prayer in the holiest motion.

Mountaineer John Muir saw a certain magnificence in this polyglot God who speaks in shout and whisper. Even a midsummer thunderstorm, "reduced to its lowest terms," he wrote, was a punctuating spectacle demanding attention, with its zigzag lances of lightning, thunderbolts "ringing like steel on steel," and then the "cataract of rain," plashing and pattering on the granite Sierra mountainside. Keeping watch from his camp in the Silver Fir woods of Yosemite Valley, he later observed, "All Nature's wildness tells the same story. Storms of every sort, torrents, earthquakes, cataclysms, 'convulsions of nature,' etc., however mysterious and lawless at first sight they may seem, are only harmonious notes in the song of creation, varied expressions of God's love."

Through the language of rain, ours is a God of endless eloquence, and whether it's love or alarm, or simply a balm, we're wise to take it all in. Even if its profoundest utterance one quiet morning is the unfettered comfort of a God who drops in via raincloud.

Is it not to begin to live sacramentally—to lift even the most ordinary moment into holiness—to fine-tune our hearing to the whole of the song of creation, to notice even the voice of the rain, the everyday sprinkling that swells open the seed, quenches the caterpillar, and refills the puddles that dimple our path?

Indeed, in the Big Book of Rain, the astonishments reach far beyond the sonic and the metaphysic. Consider these wonders of creation: there's a wild-flower, speedwell is its name, and its color is Chinese-porcelain blue; when it rains, it closes its petals to prevent its pollen from being washed away. So, too, dandelions shut their spindly umbrellas to protect their fluffy seeds from getting soaked. And farmers have long predicted rain by looking across their pastures and noticing the grass has gone "rough," when the clover—sensing moisture in the air—folds up its three little leaflets, signaling storm's on the way. Who in the heavens tends to this earth with such fine-grained attention?

And clover as weathervane is merely the start of it. According to the breathlessly titled *The Complete Weather Guide: A Collection of Practical Observations for Prognosticating the Weather, Drawn from Plants, Animals, Inanimate Bodies, and Also by Means of Philosophical Instruments*, an 1812 compendium of meteorology, folksy and otherwise, from a Brit named Joseph Taylor, frogs loom large in weather telling. If they croak more than usual, grab your umbrella; so too if toads pop up from their holes in the evening, if asses agitate their ears, if cows look to the heavens or turn up their nostrils, or if hogs shake and spoil the stalks of corn.

And let us not overlook the rain's olfactory benevolence, that unforgettable yet indescribable just-after-the-rain earthy smell. It's a smell with a name: petrichor—from the Greek *petra*, for rock, and *ichor*, the fluid in the veins of gods in Greek mythology. It's caused when rainwater mixes with certain compounds in dry soil—plant oils plus geosmin (a compound to which the human nose is highly sensitive) plus ozone, which is present if lightning's in the mix—all of which wafts into the air, and we "smell rain."

In fact, I've just stuck my nose out the door, taken a whiff, and there it is: a just-out-of-the-bath sort of a smell second only to one, the one into which I used to bury my nose when toweling dry my then-little boys, their toes shriveled like raisins, their flesh moist and pink from the tub, the occasional bubbly suds falling in dollops off their sweet curly heads. It's a heavenly wonder to think that dear God thought to perfume this weary old world—*eau de* earth just-out-of-the-bath. It's a spritz to the soul every time.

Ahh, rain. Whether droplets of water that shiver and break, or dimpling the puddles, or mimicking bottles that shatter on shelves, it is indeed nature's shapeshifter. And thus, it is God's certain way to seep in. Often intermittent, sometimes incessant, it's the dripdripdrip to the noggin: to pause and to listen, to soak in God's poem of the earth as it falls from the rainclouds, quenching this thirsty earth and all of our oft-parched souls.

Without it, we'd wither, in every which way.

WIND

Among the elements, it's the one you can't see. All we know of it comes to us secondhand; we only detect it by consequence: keeping watch on the quivering leaves, following the bounce of the tumbleweed across the dusty plain, catching the spit of the lake as it slices off top foam of waves. It's defined as air in motion, and we only hear it when it bumps up against, or blows through, the earth's musical instruments. It might howl like an oboe, or sail with a cargo of zithers. Sometimes it whines and sometimes it moans. On occasion it roars, but mostly it whispers. It is, simply, the wind. For dress-up you might deign to call it heaven's breath.

It's considered the great circulatory system of the planet, the force that through time has driven war and trade, disease and discovery. Thor Heyerdahl once noted that in the annals of adventure "man hoisted sail before he saddled a horse." It spreads life via spores and seeds, even whole surges of itty-bitty spiderlings (as any reader of dear *Charlotte's Web* might remember). It puts updraft to airborne rivers of wings, both feather and butterfly. Harnessed, it's the muscle of earth, grinds corn to meal, powers the grid, draws water from deep down below. And if not for the wind as inseminator, the immobile blooms of the earth—be they tethered to prairie or meadow or orchard, or simply your own back twenty—would have long ago gasped their last gasp, given up the whole ghost; they've only the breeze and the bees for swapping their pollens.

Planet Earth is wrapped in 5,600 million million tons of air, and most of the time most of the air is moving. It serves as our atmospheric blanket,

Goldilocks style, keeping us not too hot, and not too cold. Except for occasional outlying intemperate zones. For the most part it insulates, much like a fox's fur or the shell of a snail, only more supple, apt to adapt, to change as the wind blows. Once it gets going, the wind is inclined to reshape the landscape, sculpting wherever it goes. Sands and soils are blown hither and yon, mountainsides are smoothed and shaved over time. "Godlike, wind gives with one hand and takes away with the other," writes Nick Hunt, in the introduction to the late Lyall Watson's encyclopedic *Heaven's Breath: A Natural History of the Wind*, recounting how in the dust bowl of the 1930s, the topsoil of the American Great Plains was up and lifted, leaving behind wind hollows as deep as half a football field.

"Wind is elusive, shifty, fugitive, difficult to define—and impossible to ignore," is how it was captured by Watson, a South African "scientific nomad," who once ran the Johannesburg Zoo, before chasing after the wind and an alphabet of other subjects, from elephants to omnivores.

It's no wonder the ancients dared not ignore the wind. Early cultures worshipped wind gods and nymphs of the clouds. Pliny, the elder Roman naturalist, believed that wind, specifically the western wind, Favonius, impregnated trees. Ovid, the prolific Latin poet, envisioned each of the four winds as men either bearded and old (North and East), or young and beautiful (South and West). The Greek philosopher Anaximenes considered the swirling omnipresence of air to be proof that it was *noúmero éna* (number one) among the elements; from air, all life was breathed, and the air inside us—forever threading in and out—surely must be the soul, divine and aswirl with the life-giving breath that surrounds. The divine all around, and deep in our lungs.

It's barely a leap, then, to grasp how, from the earliest ticktock of time, wind became entwined with spirit. Its invisibility, along with its obvious force, makes it something of an indescribable mystery; in many ways, it's our first encounter with the ineffable. Have you ever watched a baby close its eyes to the wind, unsure—and often afraid—of whatever it is that's slapping its face? And then there's the basic fact that without a breath of it, we sputter and, pretty soon after, we die. From our first, we inhale it, then we keep at it for the next six or seven hundred million breaths thought to constitute a lifetime, a respiratory rate of around twenty-eight thousand breaths in a day.

"The wind is a pair of hands that encircles us," muses Jan DeBlieu, a writer and one-time coastkeeper in the Carolinas. Wind, the invisible cloak, shields us from the dark void of outer space, and it's a good bet that protective force had something to do with how its very name came to be synonymous with the Almighty: the Hebrew concept of *ruach*, the Greek *pneuma*, the Diné (or Navajo) *nilch'i*, the Iroquois *Gäoh*, and the Arabic *rūḥ*. "By wind, breath, spirit. It is all, every bit of it, the same," writes DeBlieu, in *Wind*, her 1998 meditation on how the flow of air has reshaped not only the earth but life and myth as well. In Dakota, Lakota, and Nahuatl (the language of the Aztec people), too, the word for wind and divinity are the same. Air is uncommonly sacred for the Lakota and the Diné—heaven's breath, indeed.

Those eddies and swirls of updrafting air have long fueled the sacred imagination, and the search for an image of God. In Latin, *spiritus* is defined as "the intake of breath by a god," literally an inspiration. In Hebrew, God's holiest name, a name that shall not be uttered it is so holy, is a four-letter Tetragrammaton (something like an acronym, only it's a lettered symbol reserved for one of God's names). It's composed of the most breath-like consonants in the Hebrew *aleph-bet*, Y, H, and W, combined to Y-H-W-H, which in English would read as Yahweh. Peeling it back, just a bit, and sounding it out, the first syllable, Y-H, is the inbreath, and the second, W-H, is a whispered outbreath; the whole name, a single cycle of breath. "The most sacred of God's names," writes ecophilosopher David Abram, "would thus seem to be the most breath-like of utterances—a name spoken, as it were, by the wind."

It's a sentence like that that stops me. I read it in Abram's *The Spell of the Sensuous*, a tapestry of philosophy, anthropology, and ecology written by a man who long traveled the globe as a sleight-of-hand magician, an occupational habit he now puts to work in sentences that leave me aghast. *How did he do that?* I wonder again and again. First published in 1996, Abram's book soon was considered a classic of ecophilosophy, examining the ways language is formed not just by our bodies and our communities but by the terrain and landscape that surround us. At its core, it's urgently asking how humans severed their ancient reciprocity with the natural world. And what will it take to recover a sustaining relation with the breathing earth?

It's the chapter on air, and a section on wind, breath, and speech, that has me wildly underlining, inking stars in the margins for overdone emphasis. Writing about the vast importance of breath within the Jewish mystical tradition, Abram recounts how breath was the vital substance God blew into Adam's nostrils, thereby granting "life and consciousness to humankind." Here Abram takes what feels to me like a breathtaking leap, explaining that Hebrew scribes refrained from creating distinct letters for vowel sounds, because to do so would have been to give form to the ineffable, "to make a visible likeness of the divine." Thus, vowels were left out of the Hebrew *aleph-bet* (twenty-two letters, all of them consonants). But the most sacred of God's names was compiled from a sequence of breath-like utterances.

I'd followed my way into what felt like a sacred nautilus, one hallowed chamber leading onto another, and there at the innermost apex I let out a sigh. I leapt from the page to tap out a note to one of my rabbis, Samuel Gordon is his name, and for the twenty years he's known me, he's known I am one of the curious ones, often pinging him questions, a habit we'd dubbed "Ask the Rabbi," a more deferential version of Stump the Rabbi. I sent him photos of pages 245 to 250, a modern-day book swap, and asked for his rabbinic commentary: Would he expound on Abram's breath-filled explication?

Here's what dear Sam wrote in reply: "Yes, the breath of God breathed into Adam (from *adamah*—earth) is what animates us and is, thus, the Divine in us. Fascinating to connect it to the vowels of Hebrew. The proper name of God—YHWH—is also made up of four vowel letters. It is unpronounced, but to my mind just breath/wind sounds. Imagine the sound of the wind blowing through a burning mesquite bush appearing to Moses on Sinai. God's proper name is that sound."

In a second reply, he added, "*Yod*, *heh*, and *vav* are all vowel letters [weak consonants that serve as vowels]. . . . If the Hebrew God is unknowable and God's name is unpronounceable, the name is still breath and wind which is an element that both surrounds us as wind and is internal to us as breath. Good theology there! Sam."

So it goes when you surrender to invisible currents and allow them to carry you.

In sacred stories from a shelf of holy books, the divine oft rides the wind. God bellows to Job out of the whirlwind. Sailing home from the Trojan War, Odysseus and his crew run into Aeolus, the Keeper of the Winds in Greek legend. Aeolus gives the shipmates an oxhide sack lashed with a "burnished silver cord," binding inside "the winds that howl from every quarter." It comes with strict instructions not to open it, according to Homer's epic telling. So, of course, the greedy crew unties the string, unleashing a chaotic gale that blows Odysseus wildly off course—for ten long and adventurous years. In the Gospels of Matthew, Mark, and Luke, the apostles ask themselves how it is that "even the winds and the waves obey" this force named Jesus, who with a single rebuke calms a squall on the Sea of Galilee.

Breath, the Almighty's first sigh, is wind's most intimate essence. It's ever been holy: Jesus breathes on his disciples, and, poof, the Holy Spirit is upon them; Avalokiteshvara, the Buddha-to-be of Compassion, breathes out the gift of loving kindness, and suddenly everyone can feel each other's pain. Elijah in the wilderness encounters God, not in "a mighty wind that tore mountains and shattered the rocks," but in "the sound of a gentle breeze." The Russian wanderer in The Way of a Pilgrim, the nineteenth-century spiritual classic that blew off the steppes, learns to pray ceaselessly by braiding his words with his breath, coming to believe that he and God are breathing together. To Celts, a sudden gust of air—thought to be a mischievous fairy wind—awakens a deep-down stirring, and the pious would make the sign of the cross whenever the wind blew. Hildegard, the medieval mystic of Germany's Bingen, famously taught that we should become "a feather on the breath of God," to surrender, to float, wherever the Holy Breath blows us. Brother David Steindl-Rast, a modern-day mystic, teaches that chant, like poetry, "is the wind the wind was meant to be: 'The aim was song.'" It's a reference to a charming Robert Frost poem about how the wind, blowing too hard, learns to sing, courtesy of puffed-cheek busybody bellowers. It begins, "Before man came to blow it right / The wind once blew itself untaught."

I admit to breathlessness here. But I can't seem to squelch a sense that the breadth of inspired allusion is meant to draw our attention to the one whose name, Yahweh, is the very sound of our breathing.

And then there come clouds, wind's footprint. Air, *au naturel*, is completely invisible; unlike wind, it leaves little aftermath. But add a little moisture, perhaps a water vapor so infinitesimal that "fifty billion of these tiny tears would scarcely fill a teacup," as Watson puts it, and you've got yourself a cloud. Those itty-bitty water droplets are the so-called pigment that fills in the wind's left-behind swirlings, or footprints, and suddenly the sky is cotton-puffed with atmospheric diagrams.

"Clouds were once the thrones of gods," observed art historian Kurt Badt, in a book about the English Romantic painter John Constable's canvases of clouds; "on them the angels knelt and saints took their rest." A pillar of cloud led the Jews out of Egypt, and another hovered over them in the tent of the tabernacle, when at last God revealed the glory of the Lord to his chosen ones. Such a notable accumulation was this tabernacular cloud, notes Watson, that 1,300 years later, the letter writer Paul, in his first missive to the Corinthians, thought to mention that "all our fathers were under the cloud"—of course, meaning that they were in a state of illuminated grace, not under the dark cloud of suspicion.

There are no fewer than twenty-six species of clouds; cirrus, the largest genre, have been called "eyelashes of the sun," cumulus, "fluffy cabbages in a field of summer sky," or, sometimes, "sheep grazing together at a fence line," when they cluster along the shoreline. Among the sky marvelers, there is even such a marvel as the Cloud Appreciation Society, complete with handbook, scorecard, *and* manifesto. And once upon a time, I dialed up its progenitor, Gavin Pretor-Pinney, an Englishman and amateur cloud spotter, and carried on a lofty trans-Atlantic confab that eventually migrated to email. "Magicked into being by the inscrutable laws of the atmosphere, clouds exist in a constant state of flux, shifting effortlessly from one form to another," he began in one of his follow-up dispatches from Somerset. "One moment, they're joining and spreading into undulating layers. The next, they're breaking into torn shreds. . . . And then they're gone, shedding their moisture as rain or just evaporating into the blue."

The great Scottish bard Robert Burns once wrote in his commonplace book that there was nothing that exalted, enraptured, him more than "to walk in the shelter'd side of the wood, or high plantation, in a cloudy winter-day, and hear the stormy wind howling among the trees, and raving over the plain." He called it "my best season for devotion," when his mind was "wrapt up in a kind of enthusiasm to *Him*," the one who, in the language of the Hebrew psalmist, "walks on the wings of the wind."

On the days when I hear the wind howl, especially the shiver-your-spine whistle of a blustery almost-winter day, a howl that tells you the world out your window is about to be tossed into the high-speed blender, it stops me in my tracks, whispers: *There's a force infinitely bigger than you, there's a force to lean into.*

It's the sound of something coming, the sound of batten the hatches. And sometimes it's followed by the radio squawking: winter storm's on the way. When the whistle begins, when autumn's shrill cry rattles the windowpanes, seeps in under the door, I assume lookout position: I climb into the nook that's up by the trees, take to the underside of the fuzziest afghan, press my nose to the glass. Scan the heavens for sign of storm coming.

I'll take a stiff dose of drama any old day, and the wind at trouble-making intensities certainly brings it. Shakes me into my senses. Heightens my paying attention. When you see tree trunks bending in half, posing in downward dog of the woods, you snap to salute. Wide-eyed, I begin to pray, tick through my list of most-gratefuls: for walls, between me and the wind, and for roof overhead; for a day that keeps me inside. Then, I survey my deeper-down depths. There is so much, always so much, that begs to be handed to the one who stirs the wind.

The wind, I sometimes imagine, is calling us out of ourselves, stirring the breeze deep inside, rustling up prayer. We're about to be shaken into our places again. The wind, whenever it comes, is God's deepest sigh. We're a world torn by unimaginable suffering, a world that must weary God's soul. We'd be wise to listen acutely.

And to pray right along when God's sigh comes.

FIRST SNOW

Enchanted is not a word I often put to my surrounds. But one dreamy night when I was drawn to my window, it was just that. A page borrowed from a picture book of woodland gnomes and fairies, all but waiting for one such gnome to poke his pointy cap out from under the confectioner's white-whipped swirls. It was the season's first snow, ephemeral perhaps, if the mercury rose, turned fat feather-down flakes into dollops of rain. And therein—after the long autumn's wait—is what made its beauty all the more breathtaking. It might not be long. Relish the now.

My watchkeeping began in the gloaming, as the half-tones of dusk grew inkier by the quarter hour, and at last the slate-gray skies let loose, the softening snow clouds surrendered their yield. It grew so quiet I could only imagine house after house, all in a row, noses pressed to the windowpanes, as the whole world put down its worries, quelled all its noise, to take in the falling from heaven above. Wasn't long till hard edges, sharp corners, were things of the past. All was parabola; the geometry of the curve, the math of the hour.

By bedtime, geographies were lost, all the mappings of our day-to-day traipsing obliterated under shapeless, nonangled undulations. The wind, coming in fierce against stubborn, still-clinging leaves, sounded like paper rustlings, or the crunch of stiff leather. The streetlamp cast its shadows. As would have the moon, if snow clouds hadn't occluded. The nearly full moon, shaved by one curl, was nowhere to be seen. It was quiet, squared. And motionless, except for wind in the leaves. The towering locust that looms over our roof stood sentry, unmoved by whirling snow. Arms reaching into the night, it willingly cradled whatever fell its way. Meringue mounded on every branch, every needle, every rose hip on the thorny brambles below. It would have been utterly silent, unbrokenly so, if not for the scrape of shovels from sidewalks that I couldn't see.

By morning, even at first light, my back stoop was an archeological relic of the night's woodland wanderings. I could all but picture the travels of the fat raccoon, whose star-pointed paw prints made me think this was a critter who wouldn't let a few feet of snow get in the way of a feast. He seemed to have crissed and crossed my brick steps, looking to and fro for any morsel. Either that or he was spelling out secrets in the snow. A Morse code imprinted in flakes for fellow travelers, caught unawares in the hunt for credible edibles. Poor cardinals, daunted by the billows eclipsing their seed trough, they'd taken to the drifts, making do with whatever might have blown before the snows piled on.

So it goes with the season's first snow, ablution of the loftiest order. The long-awaited rinse after the grit and the grime of the preambling months. It's the necessary pause with every first snow that I relish the most. The one time when all the world hearkens to the lifeguard's whistle, clears the proverbial pool.

The sound of snow falling and fallen is singularly soothing and startling and settling. It's the sigh after the exclamation. You might imagine, as I have, the sound of God, putting finger gently to lips, shushing. *Shhh*, you might hear God say. *Be still.*

Far from my own wintry snowfall, deep in the relict fragment of a prehistoric forest in the Scottish Highlands, where the British writer Robert Macfarlane had bundled for the night on a bed of pine boughs under a storm-felled birch, as the snows fell more and more heavily, and more and more softly, he keenly observed how "it seemed strange that so much motion could provoke so little sound." Indeed, I concurred, as I read over that particular point in Macfarlane's bewitching tale of adventures in tucked-away landscapes, from snowy wildwoods to ancient meadows, cliff tops to far-flung beaches, in his 2007 chronicle *The Wild Places*.

Turns out there's science behind the silence. Snow science. Sound absorption science, actually. And, according to the Swiss Federal Institute of Snow and Avalanche Research (the title alone lends an assurance that anyone lodged in the Alps knows a thing or two about flakes), the sound absorption rating of snow, on a scale of 0 to 1, a range of not-one-whit's absorption to can't-hear-an-ambient-note, falls between 0.87 (absorbing 87 percent of surrounding sound) for snow that's more packed, and a whopping 1.0 (absorbing 100 percent of sound) for fluffier stuff, a distinction driven by how porous are the flakes and the mounds. The snow scientists write, "Snow is considered to be a kind of sound absorbing material which consists of fine, irregular ice-particles joined together." It's the air space in and around the six-sided crystals that accounts for its stellar acoustic superpowers.

Knowing my science only magnifies the unimaginability—another word for holiest awe—I find deep in this text I'm intent on absorbing.

Henry Beston, he who stalked the wilds of Maine, seized something altogether else in the wonders of snow. "The secret of snow is the beauty of the curve. In no other manifestation of Nature is the curve revealed in an almost abstract purity as part of the visible mystery and splendor of the world." He went on to regard one snowy dune's intense, almost glowing line in the blue radiance of the morning after a snowfall, extolling the wonders of the "incomparable crest which is mathematics and magic, snow and the wind." And he marveled that "dunes of sand obey the same complex of laws, but the heavier sand does not have the aerial grace of the bodiless and radiant crystal which builds the snow against the sky." The snow is its own one-of-a-kind message from heaven.

Keeping watch on the wilds of Walden Pond, tracking the snow travels of an otter across a frozen pond (not unlike my own hungry raccoon), Henry David Thoreau famously labeled the snow "the great revealer." All the better for tracing the hieroglyphs, concealed in the undusted seasons.

Thoreau, who was quite absorbed by the unseen animator of the winter woods, turned toward the sacred when he watched the snow. In one of his January journals from 1841, he wrote that glancing up the woodsy paths, embowered by trees, was as if walking the side aisles of a cathedral, when you might "expect to hear a choir chanting from their depths." He recounted that he trod a fox's tracks, "with such a tiptoe of expectation as if I were on the trail of the Spirit itself," and watching the way the snow fell on no two trees alike, he noted how "one divine spirit descends alike on all, but bears a peculiar fruit in each. The divinity subsides on all men, as the snowflakes settle on the fields and ledges and takes the form of the various clefts and surfaces on which it lodges."

Thoreau's thinking stops me in my tracks. On my own pedestrian amblings through a wintry wood, I, like Thoreau, would surely notice the snow, and, if particularly keen-eyed one morning, I *might* zero in on the zig and the zag of some critter's gamboling. But, since I tend not to travel with track-matching guides, I'd hardly know the track of a fox from that of the neighborhood mutt loose from his leash. And chances are that would be the end of it. I'd carry on with my ambles, and my quotidian thoughts.

But not the philosopher woodsman.

Thoreau takes cogitative leaps that leave the rest of us shaking off flakes in his wake. He sees the blank sheet of snow as the tabula rasa of one wily fox whose spirit is traceable in the zigs and the zags of his woodland jaunt, and regards the paw prints left in the snow as "one expression of the divine mind." In other words, the animating divinity is perceptible if (a) you watch closely enough, and (b) you're so fluently trained to be on the lookout, you detect what most others would miss.

The insight of those long-ago theologians who espoused the Two-Book approach to divine understanding (reading in tandem the Book of Nature and the Holy Book, or, in my book, reading nature hand-in-hand with any enlightened tome) is that they understood we plebians need intellectual scaffolding to maximize our reading. It's the tension, the interplay, between the two texts—the natural and the written—that propels the deeper questions, and illuminates the connections we might not otherwise make. As long as we're here for our respective spins on the planet, why not learn to look and look closely?

Picking up on Thoreau's idea that divinity falls on each and all of us, each in our own way, I try my hand at seeing more in the winter's first snow than merely an overnight's dumping. Maybe it's this: the idea that we each in our own ways are graced by what heaven drifts upon us. And heaven knows just what it is that each of us needs—be it simply a quieting, or a chance to be blanketed in some holy comfort. It's one of those blessings we often don't realize we need until suddenly we're in the thick of it, calmed by it, soothed by it, stirred by it. That omniscience—the way the balm sometimes precedes the plea—that's what makes the surrender so necessary: God knows before we know; the answer arrives before the question is voiced.

What Thoreau seems to be suggesting is that, as snow falls ubiquitously yet takes on the form of wherever it lands, the all-knowing God brings to each of us whatever each of us needs; it quenches my thirsts, but it might whet your hungers. Snow then is the thing that we see, the visible metaphor that allows us to realize the deeper-down theological point, one that pertains to all less-physical manifestations: the hand of God is there for each of us, in a form aptly fitting. It's a thought I hold close as the snow falls. And might explain why, sometimes, as flakes somersault from the sky, I dash into the thick of it, to let a few six-spoked ice wheels plop and melt upon my shoulders, or there by my heart, absorbing whatever is their grace.

Which brings me back to the surest reason I so eagerly press my nose to the glass as the first snow tumbles, as if the angels, at last, are shaking out dust mops; the skies, soon dense with giant-size dust motes. Katherine May in *Wintering* writes that snow creates a "liminal space, a crossing point between the mundane and the magical." Maybe we're the ones who do the crossing, the snows pointing the way.

I, for one, lean into the magic there where not a branch is stirring, nor a creature in sight, once the snowfall comes to its close. It's a watercolored Bavarian woodland out there, even in my humble old plot, where every last weed, thistle, and thorn is a snow-white scrollwork. And that just might be the magic. Or, maybe, it's the miracle. The snowfall conceals, but it also reveals.

Allows us to see what was hidden. As does divinity, as Thoreau reminded; makes us see the beautiful, makes us remember it's always there, even when all we usually can see is the thorn or the thistle. And even when, especially when, the thorn or the thistle is one we sense deep down inside our very own selves. Until something comes along, falling from the heavens, perhaps, to make us see the beautiful. Deep down inside us.

It's what I've learned to be true: with every snow's first quieting, there comes an unstirrable stillness that allows us, at last, to see what's otherwise hidden. To behold the beautiful wherever it mounds.

Silently, silently so.

A LITANY OF
ASTONISHMENTS

I lifted my hands
and then my eyes
and I allowed myself
to be astonished by the great everywhere calling to me like an old
and unspoken invitation . . .

—David Whyte, Anglo-Irish poet and author

ℭ Baby birds, once hatched, memorize the night sky while still in the nest. They set their stellar compass by tracking constellations in rotation around Polaris, imprinting the heavens in their wee bird brains. Takes only two weeks for the soon-to-be navigators to know the night lights by heart. Baby birds are very busy.

ℭ There's a straightforward reason for geese flying in a chevron or vee. Each bird behind the leader is taking advantage of the lift of a corkscrew of air coming off the wingtips of the bird in front. This corkscrew updraft is called a "tip vortex." Such efficiency enables the geese to save considerable energy on long flights. We should be so energy efficient.

ℭ New research using a mini-GPS on an ibis flock has made precise measurements: birds time their wing beats so precisely that they continually catch the upwash left behind by the moving wings of the bird ahead. That means a bird regulates its stroke so its own wingtips trace the same path in the sky as the bird in front. If a bird happens to get a little closer to or farther from the bird it's following, it instantly adjusts its wing beat accordingly.

❧ And this on feathers, and how they serve as avian blankets: twenty thousand to twenty-five thousand feathers, puffed even a quarter inch, can keep a bird warmed to 104 degrees Fahrenheit.

❧ Never underestimate a bird brain: the neural capacity of the black-capped chickadee spikes in autumn, particularly in the part of the brain that stores spatial information. It grows larger and more complex to allow the chickadee to remember the exact location of seeds and insects they hide under bark and in clusters of lichen.

❧ Blue ribbon in the scatter-hoarder seed-stashing category goes to Clark's nutcracker, a crow found in the Rocky Mountains, known to gather more than thirty-three thousand pine seeds in a summer, carrying as many as one hundred at a time in a pouch under its tongue. The nutcracker, or woodpecker crow, then buries the cache in as many as five thousand sites spread across hundreds of miles, and—because of its spatial memory—is able to trace back and find the scattered treasures as long as nine months later.

❧ Just the right tool for the job: high in the Rockies, red crossbills swoop among the piney forests, perpetually on the prowl for seed-filled cones. Eons of interplay between forest and flock have custom-fitted the crossbill for conifer feasting: its stout hooked beak, a nifty utensil (think: can opener). As per its name, the crossbill's beak is, well, crossed, to make for easy access between cone scales. With a quick flick of its head, presto, the cone pops open. Add the bird's extra-long tongue: the sought-after seed deep in the cone, all but served on a platter.

THE HEAVENLY

DAWN

Sometimes I keep watch at the lakeshore, that shimmering stillwater stage from which the night curtain rises. At the lake, it's the whole picture show, the creeping edge of burning ember, from faint line to full flame in a matter of minutes. Before you know it, someone's cranked the kaleidoscope, and you're taking in colors and halos for which there's no name. Pinks and persimmon, violets and gold like its robes are on fire.

Usually, I settle in early. While it's still dark enough to make for murky outlines, I take my seat, shimmy through the sharp blades of dune grass that rise from the mounds, and make like a pheasant as I nestle in, plant my bum on the cushions of sand, grass poking up all around, a pincushion of grassy persuasion. I train my eye on the sharp straight edge, far off in the faraway. And I wait.

More often, though, I tiptoe out my own back door, and stand under the indigo bowl of the night. I step into the tableau I know best, the one fringed with the pines that made me want to buy this old house and the garden I've weeded and kneaded for nearly two decades. It's silent just before the dawn, when the veil between heaven and earth is especially thin. "For the stars close their shutters, and the dawn whitens hazily," is how Thomas Hardy penned his aubade. It's my holiest time of the day, the dayspring, the squinting hours near sunrise, just before the light comes, before the trace of familiar makes itself known. Nothing draws me into the arms of God more fully than standing here before the world starts its whisper. If ours is a God who thought to speckle the wings of the butterfly, to cross-hatch the wisps of the dandelion's mullipuff, to embroider the meadow in thimbleweed and field thistle and prairie mimosa, it's a fairly good hunch to imagine that God sees little old me, there in my bare toes or rubbery boots, wrapped in whatever I've grabbed at the door, gawking into the last vestige of night.

It's all about scale, all about understanding how evanescent this world and this life of ours is. How briefly we're here, and how little we are, us with our big giant dreams and our hopes and our infinite prayers. Sometimes that fires my soul. Makes me realize I'd better get to work. Get churning. Put grease to those gears and do those one or two things that might make a difference, might leave even a trace of a clue that I was here once, that I tried to put muscle to God's holy ask. This is the hour when I distill all my prayers, when day after day I can aim once again to lift up this day, to infuse it with God-driven purpose. Holy resurrection every time.

But that's not the only thing about dawn that draws me out from under my bedsheets. It's the silence and the stillness, the cavernous emptiness before even the first eponymous trill of the chickadee (chick-a-dee-dee-dee), the open-channel hour when the airwaves aren't yet cluttered with noise, and I stand a chance of the clearest connection—to myself, and, perhaps, to God. This is the hour when I am on my way to that voluminous quiet, the not-yet day is the time when I tell God most of my secrets. When I all but drop to my knees, begging for grace for the ones I love dearly, for the ones I know who are broken or breaking. If dawn is the hour when the sun's first light is shouldering the night aside, as one poet once pictured it, then this is the hour when I too might exercise my mightiest fibers of soul.

I wasn't always so in sync with the day's breaking out of the darkness. Once upon a time, in a children's hospital where I was a nurse, I mostly saw the first blush of light from the windows of rooms where I took care of kids sick in their beds. The kids had cancer, or any one of a dozen other deadly diseases. Kids with those sorts of terrible things tend to wake in the night. When I worked the night shift, when I was the one checking their pulse and their breathing, hooking up chemo and bringing fresh pj's, I'd sit by their side, hold their sometimes-brave, sometimes-trembling hands, and allow the words and the thoughts and the giggles to wend wherever they led.

Walking home shortly after shift change at 7 a.m., not far from Chicago's vast lakefront where by then the sky was ablaze, the morning was fuzzy and I was groggy, too groggy usually to notice. Mostly I remember walking home with the kids' unforgettable words fluttering round in my head, butterflies freed to the world.

But in the decades since, I've shimmied my way into the dawn. Now that I sleep when it's dark, the dawn is my holiest chapel.

We moved some twenty years ago into an old shingled house not far from the shoreline of Lake Michigan, in the nether land known as suburbia. We'd left behind the city and the sirens, left behind my postage-stamp-sized sanctuary, the one just off the alley where a crew from Streets and Sanitation regularly stapled "Warning: Target Rats" posters to every utility pole. In our new old house, I'd gotten to work right away carving out a meandering kitchen garden—my secret garden, as much imagination as actual footage. My unassuming plot snaked along the skinny path between our house and the wobbly fence just to the east. And that's where I took to early-morning sauntering; more like a hop and skip through my hodgepodge of plantlings and hope. A blue-slate slab, carpeted in old-house moss, fed by the drip from a downspout, offered gracious invitation for me, my coffee mug, and my morning percolations in the prayer department.

I woke early to beat the noise, to jumpstart the day—pack lunches, sip coffee, check emails, take out the trash. Back then, a night-prowling gray-striped cat served as my acolyte, meowing at the door, prompting me to leave the warm confines of a waking-up house, to step beneath the inky last drops of the night.

It wormed its way in, the dawn did. I rose earlier and earlier. It was feeding a hunger I hadn't even noticed. And all I can tell you is it chased out a demon or two, ones that had haunted and stifled for too many years. The stillness of dawn, and the depth of its prayer, at last broke the spell. And, yes, the lunches got made.

Now, my boys mostly grown—one away at college, the other not long out of law school—and no more lunches to pack, I still can't wait to meet the day.

There is something about stepping into the newness. Something about the infinite dome of those early, early hours, when the watery edge of light is just beginning to ooze across dawn's canvas. When the last of the recalcitrant stars have yet to turn themselves off, shuffle off to wherever it is the stars go to sleep.

What I know most in the awakening day is that this is when—from my moss-mottled stoop, or standing agape under the still-starry vault—it's as if I am wrapped in the most delicate prayer shawl, and I and my God are alone and entwined in the cosmos.

There are many ways to read the Book of Nature: sometimes it's a prompt, a call to prayer, a surrender to the vestibule of a single holy hour. As fixed-hour prayer constructs the architecture of attention, calling out the hours, convening the voices and soles from fields or hives or kitchens, so too time itself—the liminal hours of dawn and dusk—serves to draw us in from our domestic distractions.

And there in the stillness, in the call to attention, we just might be saved.

I'm not alone. Since the first red morning of time, from all summits and peaks, all valleys and shadowy nooks, all over this globe, something about the great star's peeking over the horizon has tugged on some holy cord deep in the human species. Maybe it's watching the dark dissolve, grain upon fine grain, or the way the colors plash on the canvas of sky, riffling clouds, rinsing light onto shapes and patterns and forms and detail that had been invisible just minutes before. It's almost as if we're hard-wired for awe. And so, the dawn's been anointed, enwrapped in the liturgical, sanctified as the holy hour, devoted to praise, often in chant or in song.

Every Abrahamic religion has written the day's rising of light into its prayer code, beginning with the ancient Judaic command to consecrate the new day with the *Birkot Hashachar*, fifteen blessings for the dawn spelled out in the Talmud, starting with thanks to God for the rooster's "ability to distinguish between day and night."

In Islam, the muezzin keeps watch for the first crack of light on the eastern horizon, and beckons all believers to the dawn prayer, the *Fajr*, technically the day's third call to prayer since the Islamic day begins at sundown. The holy chant unfurls from the earliest suffusion of light until the solar disc crosses the horizon, a praise prayer to Allah, Most Gracious, Most Merciful.

In Christian monastic fixed-hour prayer, when the night vigil ends and the cloister walls echo in the day's first antiphons, the sacred pause is called lauds, the coming of the light. Brother David Steindl-Rast, the Benedictine monk with the worldwide gratefulness flocks, distills the holy message of lauds to the notion that each sunrise, each new beginning, is a never-ending gift. In turn, in response to this unasked-for benevolence, our reciprocity is to ask ourselves, "What gift might I bring to this day?" He turns our attention to a beautiful Rainer Maria Rilke poem in *The Book of Hours*, one that might have been written just for lauds, a poem that Steindl-Rast likens to something of a creation myth. The poet imagines God speaking to each of us as God makes us, before we are born, and before we leave the womb of darkness. Rilke writes that God "walks with us silently out of the night." And as we move closer to the edge, to where the light's coming in, God whispers,

> Let everything happen to you: beauty and terror.
> Just keep going. . . .
> Don't let yourself lose me.

The three final lines are these:

> Nearby is the country they call life.
> You will know it by its seriousness.
> Give me your hand.

And so we pray at the edge of the day's holy light. *Let me not let go, God. Don't let me let go.*

In the rocky outposts of Ireland, and the wind-haunted Scottish isles, the Celts took their dawn with a similar hushed reverence. Before Christianity infused their beliefs, it was thought that the morning's dew held potent powers of healing, and you'd be all the wiser to roll in it. Especially so at Beltane, the midpoint between vernal equinox and summer solstice, a feast of fertility, when the peat was thought to glisten in high-energy dew, and to rinse your face in a bowl of it was a good bet to bring you the fairest of fair complexions.

Even once the Celts layered on Trinitarian tenets, the liminal space between darkness and light was one wrapped in piety, albeit in the simple vernacular of a hardworking people.

God was considered "the Sun behind all suns," as the author George MacLeod once wrote. The whole of creation was dappled with the light of the sun as it journeyed across the sky. Wherever its light fell, there was God filtering through, an earthly translation of the divine infusion. And the perpetual Celtic praise song rose up with the dawn. Celtic gentlemen—farmers and herders and fishermen, set off to work in the predawn darkness—doffed their hat at the first light of the sun, and bowed in blessing. The *Carmina Gadelica*, a collection of Gaelic prayers and chants, is filled with start-of-day blessings, as the Celts were wont to offer up benediction for every chore and implement and God-given element of every day, from milking to weaving to shearing the sheep, from fire to wind to sprinkling of water. And certainly for the miraculous return of the morning's first light. Mystic and teacher Alexander Scott, who grew up in the west of Scotland and kept Celtic ways alive in his nineteenth-century books, wrote that his were a people "listening for God in all things, 'in the growth of the tree, in the rising of the morning sun, in the stars at night, and in the moon.'"

Sometimes even poetries can't capture creation's inexpressibility. We turn then to the painters and sculptors and makers of music whose work begins where words trail off. I recently found myself lost in a painting, oil and graphite on linen titled *Golden Dawn*, by the American abstract expressionist Richard Pousette-Dart, who once called his religion his art, and his art his religion. Like its muse, the hour when the world rises out of darkness, the canvas explodes with luminosity, as if the gold daubed from the palette is surging forth from some celestial force, yet it's misted in a fog like so many a daybreak. Indecipherable are graphite pencilings traced throughout, again reminiscent of the way the thin light of dawn, grain by grain, brings form to that which the night hides. It reminds me that to stare into the dawn can be a sublime meditation, as if looking into a living icon of God, drawing us out of our everyday consciousness, into the untapped depths of the mysterious sacred light that's within.

Thomas Merton, who called the first light "a moment of awe and inexpressible innocence," as the birds in the bough begin their tentative chirping and an ashen moon departs, railed against inattention to dawn's beckoning: "Here is an unspeakable secret: paradise is all around us and we do not understand. It is wide open. The sword is taken away, but we do not know it: we are off 'one to his farm and another to his merchandise.' Lights on. Clocks ticking. Thermostats working. Stoves cooking. Electric shavers filling radios with static. 'Wisdom,' cries the dawn deacon, but we do not attend."

O Lord, let us attend. Let us not lose the taste of its spell, not one droplet of this holiest hour.

DUSK

I t's the liminal hour, the gloaming, "a time that is not a time," the Celts call it. It's the hour when night enfolds the day, and the grainy darkness begins to settle in. It's the hour when the night orchestra—cricket, katydid, maybe even peepers if you're not far from a soggy place or a pond—warms up its fiddles and throats. It's the fluid hour, too; waiting patiently off in the wings till well past suppertime, come summer, but not so in wintertime. Winter is when the dusk is impatient, likes to get an early start. Arrives just as the afternoon teakettle whistles. And as with all interminglings, we humans are drawn to it. Curious. We imbue it with meanings and poetries. I suppose it's hard to ignore the pageant of it, off in the western sky, when the slipping-away sun seems to explode, leeches all across the canvas in raspberry and tangerine colors, sometimes streaks aubergine, just for the art of it. A whole produce cart spilled across the sky.

"Some sort of carnival magician has been here, some fast-talking worker of wonders," is how Annie Dillard saw it, watching the show from the banks of Tinker Creek. Walt Whitman, taking in sundown from the New Jersey country-side, scribbled this in his 1878 journal: "This is the hour for strange effects in light and shade—enough to make a colorist go delirious—long spokes of molten silver sent horizontally through the trees (now in their brightest tenderest green,) each leaf and branch of endless foliage a lit-up miracle . . . in ways unknown to any other hour." Edgar Allan Poe insisted he could hear the night darkness, as it poured, in the evening, into the world, "each separate dying ember wrought its ghost upon the floor." T. S. Eliot pronounced dusk "the violet hour."

And while the poets have romps in it, it's the pietists who most deeply stir me. The sacred veil of twilight—a word derived from "two lights," the mystical time of encounter between visible and invisible, when the time of the sun marries the time of the moon—is lifted just enough for the holy to come rushing in. It's in the thresholds, the murky edges of time, when the ancient Celts—and likely all those attuned to such subtle spiritual shiftings— perceived more palpably a presence usually beyond reach. Put simply, as the Celts put it, the spirits could "get through" in the gauzy hours. At twilight, after a long day's toil, imagination lets down its guard, and the heightened permeability meant intermingling of heaven and earth. For proof that these in-between times pumped potent energies into the world, the Celts point to birdsong, amplified in the bedtime hour, when the feathered choristers put aside their worldly concerns and let loose their God-given nocturnes.

In the plainsong of my evening encounters, it's simply the dimming, the quieting at the end of the day that becalms me. I never mind the invitation to draw in, to enter a coil of time that unfurls in dialed-down tempo, adagio. Is it a stretch to wonder if God dims the lights to turn our attention beyond the hubbub of the everyday, to call us from bodily labor to that of the soul?

And never so much as the dusk at the end of the work week, at the cusp of Shabbat, when, in Jewish law, all the madness comes to a halt, and, as the late great rabbi Abraham Joshua Heschel once wrote, we "lay down the profanity of clattering commerce, of being yoked to toil," when we "go away from the screech of dissonant days."

In fact, we're commanded: remember the Sabbath day, and keep it holy.

Re-creating the first declaration of Genesis, we kindle the flame just before sundown on Fridays, and let there be light. So begins the Jewish Sabbath, the great cathedral of time in Judaism, the holy of holies that "neither the Romans nor the Germans were able to burn," as Heschel most pointedly put it. It is a sanctified time in which to mend our tattered lives, to enter into nothing less than holiness.

God blessed the seventh day, and hallowed it.

Oh, do I need it.

I couldn't tell you the first time I pulled out the pair of silver filigreed Shabbat candlesticks or the kiddush cup, both from an Israeli market, wedding gifts from the widow of one of my husband's closest college friends, a brilliant human-rights lawyer who'd died far too young. But I do know that first Shabbat, just my husband and I at our old maple table, wasn't long after we married. And it's become a perpetual rhythm in this old house.

Over the decades, I've tried my hand at rising early on Fridays to sift flour; whisk oil and yeast, eggs and a wee pinch of sugar; to stir and knead and let rise the pillowy mound of what would be the evening's challah. But mostly my braids emerged from the oven looking reptilian. More than once, like something akin to a lobster with menacing claws. I even enlisted the tutelage of a Holocaust survivor who, by telephone, walked me step-by-step through his three-page instructions. These days, we buy. And even though we've been known to forget the challah—foraging in the pantry instead for any starchy foodstuff, even a Triscuit or handful of popcorn—we never forget to bring to the table the hand-painted challah covers long ago labored over by both of our boys at the Jewish-Catholic Sunday school where all of us learned to be versed in both our religions.

Shabbat, a sanctification at dusk, is one of our treasures, an interlude I've come to count on, to sink into its heavenly folds, week after week. It's a call to attention timed to begin when the sun slips at last beneath the horizon, a time that for years was spelled out on the front page of the *New York Times*, with a small ad that each Friday listed the precise moment to light the *Shabbos* candles, eighteen minutes before sundown, an instruction meant to ensure that, at least among readers of the *Times*, not a single Jew would tarry and miss even a fraction of a minute of Shabbat's holy hours.

Set off by the celestial lights that divide the day and the night, separate ordinary time from that which is sacred, Shabbat is a sanctuary arising from the architecture of time. Every hour of every day is anointed, yet never so holy as the hours that arc from sundown to sundown on the day we remember God's holy creation.

But even on an ordinary weekday, the dimming hour summons the sacred.

In monasteries encircling the globe, the half-tones of dusk mark the time when the bells ring for vespers, the lighting of the evening lamp, amid the chanting of evensong. The blessing of the evening lamp is thought to be the ancestor of *Lucernarium*, an ancient cathedral service when candles were lit for both practical and spiritual purposes, and incense was burned, symbolizing prayers rising to heaven. In the sixth century, elements from the solemn *Lucernarium* were spread across evening prayer, vespers, and night prayer, compline, as two separate contemplative hours. Brother David Steindl-Rast, the Benedictine monk, calls vespers—when a monk's tools are put away, work clothes traded for tunics tied with a knot—"the hour of peace of heart, of serenity." It's the time for the reconciling of the day's contradictions—those within us, and those around us. At vespers, the great prayer of the Magnificat is chanted, the song from Saint Luke's Gospel when Mary, the mother of Jesus, greets her cousin Elizabeth, proclaiming the greatness of the Lord. Whether Anglican, Catholic, or Orthodox vespers, the chanting of the Blessed Mother's prayer is the liturgical highpoint, as the altar is incensed, and all face toward the east, consecrating the coming of nightfall. In all, the kindling of candlelight, the chanting, the softening shadow, it makes for the day's great exhalation and the in-breath of sacred. Our godly work, our *opus Dei*, writes Steindl-Rast, is to imagine how we might bring light into this dark world. It's a question I ask, over and over.

Over the millennia, the monasteries, with their vigilance to time and cosmos, have infused the rhythms of day and night, dawn to dusk to midnight, with a seamless sacramentality, often punctuating the hours with borrowings from pages of the Book of Nature. And so, it's at once breathtaking yet hardly surprising to learn that at the close of the night's prayer, the abbot sprinkles the prayerful with holy water, "a sort of evening dew," writes Brother David. And thus the night watch—the Great Silence—begins deep within the cloister.

Jews, commanded to pray all through the day and into the night, but especially at the margins of time—the beginnings and ends of allotments of hours or seasons—gather just after sunset for *Maariv*, the prayer of the One "who brings on twilight," as is the Hebrew translation. "Holy is twilight—the realm of in-between. And so our sages taught: pray in the moments when light and darkness touch," writes Rabbi Reuben Zellman, in the *Mishkan Halev*, a prayer book for the month before the Jewish Days of Awe, the ten high holy days of every autumn. He goes on to pray, "May the sacred in-between of this evening suspend our certainties, soften our judgements, widen our vision. Let it illumine our way to the God who transcends all boundaries and definitions. Blessed are You, God of all, who brings on the twilight."

Islamic prayer, too, pours across the hours of the day, directed by the sun, with five calls to prayer from sunrise until after sunset. In the evening, Muslims are called to *Maghrib*, the sunset prayer, which actually marks the beginning of the day, followed by *Ishaa*, the late evening prayer. Muslim prayer demands close watch on the celestial stirrings. The sunset prayer begins only when the disc of the sun has dropped fully below the horizon, a time when evening stars begin to fill the night sky, and the evening prayer lasts, according to most but not all Muslim scholars, until the last red thread of light disappears from the horizon's edge, marking the beginning of *Ishaa*. It is, as with the evening prayers of most traditions, a song of praise and confession, a cleansing from the day, and an entering into the sacred of the long night's silence.

It's not hard to imagine how this darkening hour captured the wide-eyed attention of those in the ages before lightbulb or even beeswax candle. The singular solar orb slipped away, vanished off the edge, its pilgrimage across the sky come to a close. A daily occurrence likely to strike terror in those keeping watch. We, in all our modernities, now know that it's geometry and light physics combined, as the rays of the sun scatter through the upper atmosphere, illuminating the lower atmosphere. The earth's surface is neither completely lit nor dark, and the western sky is ablaze in tongues of flame. Roger Deakin, in *Wildwood*, laments that in our plugged-in era, with our endless strings of streetlights and our off-the-charts kilowatt hours, we're all but missing the dusk, "the time of darkling shades in which our pupils can dilate by slow degrees and dreams drift in as, wide-eyed, we enter the rook-black night."

We'd be wise to not let it slip by unnoticed. The poet Patricia Lunetta makes the point poignantly in her poem "The Visit," in which, after a long day at a dying friend's bedside, she pulls onto the gravel shoulder of a narrow curving road, and, near nightfall, catches sight of a great blue heron, "like a priest in feathered robes." Bowing its head three times before "an altar of mountain bluffs," with the moon just rising, the heron spreads its wings, illuminated, "in benediction for evening flight." Its parting call, the poet imagines, "Stay awake, Holiness may spread its wings for you at any moment."

Stay awake, indeed. The hallowed eventide beckons.

I don't always wander outside in wintertime's twilight, but inside the walls of my old creaky house, I wrap myself in the hour's sacramental invitation. It's when I'm apt to kindle a candle or three, and crank the stove, my own ancient altar of simmering incantation. I never mind the encroaching darkness, feeling cradled in its blanketing, knowing it's a call to my own follow-me-everywhere interior monastery. In summer, I can't stay away from our old screened porch, where I plop my bum in the wicker chairs, and await the in-beaming light, bathing the garden in something like gold dust. It's never long till the cricket song arises—Nathaniel Hawthorne's "audible stillness"—and, plenty soon, the stars and the fireflies begin their flickering.

I whisper the words of William Wordsworth, words I oft heard from my mother, who punctuated the day, from sunup to sundown, with her by-heart recitations, and held a particular fondness for the English Romantics:

> It is a beauteous evening, calm and free,
> The holy time is quiet as a Nun
> Breathless with adoration.

I am quiet. Yes.

STARS

I 've never made it much past the Big Dipper. I'm a remedial reader. Of the night map, anyway. Even H. A. Rey, he who gave the world Curious George, tried to get in on the act, to throw me a tutorial, show me the heavens in simple pictorial shapes, ditching earlier connect-the-dots of geometric or allegorical proportion, which until Rey had pretty much been the stargazer's way. Simple truth is: I take my stars en masse, go dizzy for their teeny fragments of lucence, pin dots in the night cloth; it's all a barely discernible whirl, as I stand there, neck bent back, eyes on the skies, tracing invisible lines. But when it comes to delighting in heavenly wonders, I am indeed off the charts.

Rey, a stargazer of astronomical heights, devoted a good chunk of his drawing life to penciling in the shapes he saw in the sky, a whole carousel, really, a celestial zoo: giraffe and bear, lion and fox, bull and ram and fishes. Even a lizard he saw in the sky. And a unicorn, too. The German-born illustrator, who escaped the Nazis (and who for a short stint in his storybook life sold bathtubs in Brazil, along the Amazon River) wanted little more than to inspire a next generation of gazers of nighttime's picture show. In his 1952 book, *The Stars: A New Way to See Them*, a book I've long had on my shelves, he advocated more common names—the Twins, Bears, Whales—instead of the vowel-jammed Latin ones—Gemini, Ursa, Cetus—that would trip up beginners. And he spent the next 141 pages mapping the heavens in easier-to-read dot-to-dot pictures. If only he'd drawn that mischievous monkey up high in the sky. We might all be more curious when it comes to tracing the night lights.

Truth is, though, the fascination with stars is ancient. The first traces of starry attraction date back some six thousand years to the early Egyptians, Chaldeans, and Sumerians. For millennia, stars have charted the way: sailors crossed seas by them, farmers sowed fields, adventurers crisscrossed the land, and we know that America's enslaved people followed the drinking gourd to freedom. The name for the science of charting the heavens is *uranography*—from the Greek for "heaven or sky writing," aka celestial cartography. And, apparently, it didn't take long for early uranographers to begin to read lessons in the sky.

The constellations—seeing shapes, making sense of what might seem a blur—have been called humankind's oldest picture book, even if the first lessons were drawn five thousand years ago with sticks in the Babylonian sand. The Babylonians were the first to tell sky stories, dividing the heavens into chapters, the twelve zodiac signs. According to Hebrew Scripture, Yahweh counted the stars, and gave a name to each one. Plato posited that our souls came from the stars, and to the stars they shall return. Ancients broadly thought the stars to be gods and goddesses swifting through the night. Venus, both morning star (considered masculine) and evening star (feminine), was paid particular attention by virtue of his and her riveting brilliance, a star so bright you could see it with a naked eye, no telescope needed. Early Greeks, under the tutelage of Plato, believed the stars were living beings. Pythagoras, the geometrician of many angles, argued that if you listened closely enough in the night you could hear a celestial song, one he named *musica universalis*, and he insisted that all of the heavenly bodies—sun, moon, planets, and each of the stars—hummed their own tune. If only he'd shown the math to prove it.

Now, if left to my own night-watching rudiments, I might stare at the stars till the lights fizzle out and, other than glimmer and wonder, not see too deep into the darkness. But when I turn to the star guides, the ones in the books on my shelves, the ones in my star-studded roster, I discover a cosmos otherwise opaque to me. The constellations of insight there on the page give me the scope I need to see more, to connect dots and stellar ideas.

The ancients, in particular, fine-tune my focus, as I consider the potency they imbued in the stars. (*Consider*, literally, "think with the stars," *con* [with] + *sideris* [heavenly body]; and, along that very etymological vein, *desire*, "longing for something you cannot reach," derives from the same Latin roots, "away from the stars.")

Once upon a time, the world went dark every night, obsidian dark, except for the lights that blinked on in the heavens. Theirs was a darkness unlike most any we've seen in our lives. And yet the ancients found their way, scoping pinpoints of stardust, with only the flame of the heavens pointing the way. Pulled by those improbable lights in the inkiest dome, stories were gathered and volumes of myth. The night was bejeweled in their eyes, the Great Winter Hexagon (the six brightest points in the Northern Hemisphere's winter nights), described as "the jeweled face of God."

It's kindling those sorts of thoughts—thoughts extracted from pages of books—that ignites my fieriest imagination, opens wide for me whole tracts of starry contemplations. But even more so, makes me want to tiptoe into the night, to begin to imagine such faith and such fluency in the heavenly lamps that we in our twenty-first-century stupors so little notice. Are we moderns the ones who've lost our way?

We barely look up anymore, no longer ask questions of heavens, now that we've so busied our lives, polluted our globe not just with smog and noise and the usual twenty-first-century sins. We've polluted *ourselves* with distraction; all the wonderments, wasted. We might live our whole lives—or even just stretches of years—without ever once looking to find Cassiopeia pert on her throne, or planting our bum on a log, keeping watch for kamikaze stars.

By turning to books, the collected inquiry of countless curious minds searching for clues to the cosmos's mysteries, even a remedial gazer like me can begin to make deeper sense of what's above and beyond not only our reach but our farthest-flung thoughts.

The point here is that sometimes our inquiries needn't be solo expeditions. In setting out to canvass the cosmos we might bump into the occasional black hole: we can sit and stare and see not very much, or we can turn to navigational guides and peek over the shoulders of glorious minds who've been watching and seeing for all of their lives. Be it stars or planets or the ways trees shed their leaves.

And perhaps the point is to live in perpetual question, as Meister Eckhart more or less encouraged. But even if we never peek under the hood of nature's inner workings, even if we never consider even a fraction of all there is to stir up our wonder and our wondering, all the cosmos stands ready to draw us in to its endless bedazzlement. So I look to the stars.

Star science, it seems, is rather straightforward: hydrogen + helium, massively balled; nuclear fusion burns at the core. It all started with the Big Bang, 13.8 billion years ago, when untold numbers of bits—think heavenly cinders—kaboomed into the black canyon of space. The number of stars: more than a billion trillion. The starlight we see from down here below, it's taken eight minutes to get here from starry explosion. Oh, and stars, by the way, come in colors, and, yes, they're red, white, and blue. Blue are the giants, red ones are cooling, and white are considered the dwarfs. A black hole is when a star caves in on itself, a phenomenon described as "gravitational collapse." And the geniuses who measure these things tell us that every minute on a square mile of turf, one ten-thousandth of an ounce of starlight drizzles onto that little plot of earth. (Less poetic astrophysicists, when quantifying the starlight that sputters upon us, put it prosaically: it's more like a 60-watt lightbulb—seen from 2.5 miles away, in complete darkness.) I have a hard time picturing that, either way, but I like the idea of a gentle rain of stardust sprinkling down. Which reminds me: I'm told, by star-seers who know, that *we* are made of actual stardust and that all the atoms and elements in our whole selves—as well as the entire periodic table of elements, the building blocks of all chemistry—come from generations of stars and supernova burning to dust and filtering down, a star-dusting that's lasted for the past 4.5 billion years.

It's wonder, in very bright lights.

And for anyone born to a world where night after night the stars turn on, as if the caretakers of wonder have soared through the heavens, sparking the star-wicks with their long-necked matches, it's all but impossible to take our eyes off the infinite dome. It's "an abyss timeless and remote and sown with an immense glittering of stars in their luminous rivers and pale mists, in their solitary and unneighbored splendors, in their ordered figures, and dark, half-empty fields," wrote Henry Beston, a poet if not a certified uranographer, as he stood under the night's winter sky in 1948 on his farm in Maine, not far from the Atlantic Seaboard.

It's an alchemical mix, the elemental plus the infinite that equals the awe. And it's ever been. Pattiann Rogers, in her poem "On the Existence of the Soul," asks,

> And if not for its sake, why would I go
> out into the night alone and stare deliberately
> straight up into 15 billion years ago and more?

The night is "alive with lamps," wrote the poet Edward Hirsch, in *Wild Gratitude*, in a poem whose title alone is a poem, "In Spite of Everything, the Stars." Roger Deakin, the British tramper with one of the keenest visions that ever there was, commented, "Strange how beautiful sky-litter can be." Annie Dillard lamented all that we miss, from shooting stars to meteor showers, writing, "they're out there . . . committing hara-kari in a flame of fatal attraction . . . but at dawn what looks like a blue dome clamps down on me like a lid on a pot." Stars and planets might be smashing out there, and we'll never know. And maybe it's that cloak of mystery, the infinite unchartedness that holds the allure.

How can it be that heaven's cloths could be so embroidered, "enwrought with golden and silver light," as William Butler Yeats so noted, and we are left with only our wonder? Maybe that's the point. Maybe it's the divine suggestion that we'll never get to the ends of our searching, never reach the far reaches of faraway. Maybe the estuaries of heaven are meant to lure us up, up, and away.

John Calvin, more of a sensualist than his stiff-spined reputation would have you believe, wrote that astronomy might be called "the alphabet of theology." It launches the wildest, most otherworldly questions.

One of the first theologians to extract wisdom from the night's great mystery was Origen of Alexandria, the third-century truth seeker, who found himself fascinated by the Platonic notion that the stars were alive. He argued there was a star-like quality in each and every human, writing, "You must understand that you are another world in miniature, and that there is in you sun and moon and also stars. . . . You to whom it is said that you are 'the light of the world.'" Origen is telling us the human soul is a mirror of that which we see in the sky's ceaseless shimmer, and it's all a vast allegory of the divine. It's God's luminescence that shines in the stars. Or as the ancient Celts, deeply influenced by Origen, would distill it, the lights that shine from out of the darkness "express something of the inexpressible." We should reach for the stars.

And sometimes we're guided by stars. And not merely in an earthly plodding sort of a way, plotting point-to-point on a map. Rather, navigations of the soul-stretching sort. The three magi, of course, leap to mind, the stars of the Epiphany story, ancient travelers trekking foreign terrain, seeking destination unknown, led by radiant light and unswervable hunch. It's a story that's always held me rapt, and not merely because I was born in its halo, three days before the Catholic Church's January 6 celebration of the magi. In the ages-old story, the three (an old and beloved hymn refers to them as kings, but scholars now believe they were probably astronomers), guided only by night star, set out with their rarest of spices and gold to behold the newborn babe in the manger. I, too, find much to behold. At the dawn of the new year, in the stillness that follows the Yuletide folderol, we, like the wise ones, might scan our own heavens, plot our own course, muster the courage to take the first step. And the next, and the next. Years ago, I was gathered in a classroom listening to Renaissance scholar and poet Kimberly Johnson, when she spoke eight words I instantly pressed to my heart: "I want to live my life in epiphany." So do I. So, maybe, do you.

There's a lesser-known story, a charming story, told by Belden Lane in *The Great Conversation*, of a desert monk in Spain hundreds of years ago, who each day was sent to beg in a far-off city. His cross-desert journey was long, and his thirst grew with each footstep. God, so the story goes, marveled at the monk's faithfulness and decided to create a thirst-quenching well along his path. The monk refused to take even a sip, offering it up as gesture of honor to God. Each night when the monk lay in his bed, he looked out the window of his cell, and night after night, there shone a single star in the sky. This, the monk imagined, was pinned there by God, a sign of God's great gratitude. And so it went the monk's whole life long, till his last day on earth. That day, the old monk had brought along a young monk to teach him the beggarly ways. As ever, the drinking well appeared, and this time the young monk gulped down a swig; the old monk, though, was torn, not wanting to drink, but not wanting to appear "holier than thou" by refusing. At last, the old monk took the drink, awash in regret, worried that God would not be well pleased. When he lay down that night, and peeked out his cell's window, the old monk feared there'd be not a star. But what he saw was a whole sky stippled in starlight. That night, the old monk died in his sleep, a most peaceful sleep, it's been said. The moral of the story, writes Lane, is that mercy is better than sacrifice. Strict asceticism can't beat compassion. "Love alone is what shows you the face of God. It's what makes the stars shine."

Such are the illuminations that come from the stars—if only we look up to notice.

In my own astral history, the stars that have stirred me most unforgettably are the ones to which I've been pointed by the commands of the Torah, the holy book that for me profoundly connected the dots between the divine and the dance of the cosmos—or made me see most abundantly clearly that God's first holy text, the Book of Nature, wasn't just pages of "pretty," but rather an exquisitely writ volume of wisdoms and truths that beg to be plumbed. In the Hebrew Bible, at the harvest festival of Sukkot, when we're called to dwell under the heavens for a stretch of eight days in a booth or a hut of our own making, a remembrance of the exodus, the Jews' fleeing from Egypt when "clouds of glory" shielded them in the Sinai Desert, it is no less than a commandment that through the roof of the structure—called a *skhakh* in Hebrew—we should be able to see the stars. The point, I do believe, is that God wants us to wrap ourselves in God's wonder. Do not dismiss the divine sparks of light all around, in this case the ones stitched into the black velvet of nighttime. In all my years in churches, I'd not been told so directly (nor exquisitely) to enfold myself in the adornments of God's holy earth. Or at least not that I remembered, and it was an epiphany that caught my breath. That God so intricately instructs, points us toward the doors to the heavens. It's an attention to wonder found again and again in the rhythms of Judaism, rhythms now woven into my own everyday, although mine is a weave of many threads. At the close of Shabbat, that once-weekly command to take holy pause, to sanctify time outside of time, Jews are told to watch for three evening stars, and only then should the wick of the braided *havdalah* candle be kindled, and the spice box passed under our noses as we unfurl the blessings of the just-ended Sabbath and the holiness of the week newly unfurling.

And maybe all of that is why the words of Abraham Joshua Heschel come spilling to mind: "He who has ever been confronted with the ultimate and has realized that sun and stars and souls do not ramble in a vacuum will keep his heart in readiness for the hour when the world is entranced, and awaits a soul to breathe in the mystery that all things exhale in their craving for salvation. For things are not mute. The stillness is full of demands. Out of the world comes a behest to instill into the air a rapturous song for God, to incarnate in the stones a message of humble beauty, and to instill a prayer for goodness in the hearts of all children."

To that, I whisper *Amen*. I'll be watching next time the heavens trot out the stars.

MOON

In the house where my boys grew up, the one where I clanged the pans, kept everyone shod, they learned early on to keep watch of the nightlight, the one orb in the sky you could watch with your own bare eyes. If I was the teacher, old Mr. Moon was the ancient professor. Instruction began well before kindergarten, when I'd bundle us up and allow for whatever equipment and armament was petitioned. Purple plastic spy binoculars came in handy. As did pockets filled with Cheez-Its and animal crackers. And, for a while there, and for reasons that only make sense to five-year-old boys, light sabers came too, in various sizes and superpowers. Sometimes we took in our lessons by foot, the appropriately labeled moon walk. Sometimes we took to the beach, where blankets were spread as the night fell. Sometimes we gazed from only our windows. The lessons, ancient and elemental instruction in addition, subtraction, and slivers of fractions, were only the start of it. What mattered more was that my boys were learning to marvel, learning how little we are in the whirl of the cosmos, learning to read the pages of heavens. Ours was a curriculum as old as all time.

That nightly infusion of borrowed light, the sponge in the sky soaking up whatever the sun has to spare, it's been ordering lives and religions, starring in myths and origin stories, pulling the tides as well as our prayers, infusing the lore of farmers and herders and poets, since all the way back to Day Four of creation. You'd not be mistaken to think it the crux of celestial enchantment—and myriad puzzlement. It's been labeled the "orb imperial," that smudge of chalk that swells and shrinks in the night sky. Walt Whitman wondered if there was so much as a mote of lunar landscape that hadn't been trampled (often clumsily) in the pages of poetry or literature. And then he went on to quote an 1878 *New-York Tribune* column that waxed of the moon, "Goddess that she is by dower of her eternal beauty, she . . . knows the charm of being seldom seen, of coming by surprise and staying but a little while; never wears the same dress two nights running, nor all night the same way." The bard's not done, unable to wane the waxing: Luna, the name the Romans pinned to the moon, "lends herself to every symbolism and to every emblem; is Diana's bow and Venus's mirror and Mary's throne; is a sickle, a scarf, an eyebrow, his face or her face, as look'd at by her or by him; is the madman's hell, the poet's heaven, the baby's toy, the philosopher's study; and while her admirers follow her footsteps, and hang on her lovely looks, she knows how to keep her woman's secret—her other side—unguess'd and unguessable." No wonder dear Luna sometimes shrinks into darkness; how else to keep the howlers at bay?

In the moon stories of my own history—the nights I've played peekaboo with a cheddar wheel of harvest moon, one that in its early ascent seemed to hide and peek behind treetops as I raced to the lakeshore to catch its rising, the nights I've tiptoed outside in my nightgown and slippers for no other reason than to dance in the moon lace, the Chantilly of shadow that stipples the yard when moonbeams, mid-hurl to the ground, find themselves nipped and tucked by the leaves and the boughs of the trees that get in the way—the one I hold most unflinchingly is the one when the unseen moon preaches its sermon on faith. It goes something like this: just because you can't see the heavenly light on a particularly cloud-crowded night, doesn't mean it's not there—a wisdom I liken to the truth of the God I've not yet looked in the eyes. I've had nights on moon watch—not the headline-stealing spectacles, not lunar eclipses, not once-in-a-zillion-years sky show, just your basic every-night astonishing moon rise—when it's gotten so quiet, so still, so steeped in spine-tingling awe as the great silver ball glides up the skydome that I half expect, standing alone on the beach, to turn and see another pair of footprints there in the sand beside me; the footprints of God, of course.

I remember one particular moonless night, a Shabbat when my prayers felt so big, and the answers so distant, instead of going off to the synagogue I made my way to a sanctuary of endless proportion, where the reach is forever and there are no walls. I went to the edge of the shoreline, where cottonwoods finger the darkness, and dune grasses make for fine pews. That night, uncannily, the lake made no sound. Stillness abounded, eerily so. And the moon, a moon I knew to be practically full, was nowhere in sight. Out of the silence, out of the pitch-black darkness, a lone goose wailed a dissonant dirge. But I couldn't see it. Nor sliver of moon. Couldn't hear a ripple of lake, nor the flapping of faraway wings. And that's when it hit me, the knowing I'll never forget: just because I couldn't see or hear or sense any presence, it didn't mean it wasn't there. The lake in its stillness was where it belonged; the goose, high in the night; the moon, even higher. And the God to whom I was praying, God was there too. Certainly, knowingly. Absent of proof.

Proof, in the realm of omniscience, is elusive, proof of the knowledge of God is why we rely on our senses. All creation offers limitless sense.

It's a knowing I now carry with me. It's one of the accumulated ones I've gathered along the way, ever since I began to take my theological lessons from the holiest book I know, the one spelled out in moonbeams and the cry of the night-crossing goose. I've found those lessons, the ones that come through my eyes or my ears or my flesh and not merely my brain, to be unerasable. Like all learning, knowing is built layer by layer. And one indelible night under the moon is a night that now never leaves me.

Nor its truth.

In the annals of history, ancient and otherwise, the charms of the moon abound, as Whitman alluded. Given its nightly installments against the backdrop of darkness, the way it all but cries out, *Watch me, watch me*, it's little wonder it stars in so many sense-making stories. To the Luhya people of Kenya in East Africa, the sun and moon were brothers. Moon was older, bolder, and bigger, and the lesser sun was jealous and picked a fraternal fight. As the two wrestled, the moon fell in the mud, dimming its brightness. God quelled the squabble and settled the matter, assigning each orb to its own separate shift. Sun was to shine by day, and the mud-splattered moon was to light the night, thought by the Luhya to be the world of witches and thieves. An old Indigenous legend of the moon and the locust tree (found in both Cherokee and Iroquois lore, with slight variations) goes like this: the moon goddess starts out with a big ball, the full moon, which she heaves across the sky. She spends all day fetching it, then shaves off a slice and heaves it again, day after day, one moon per month, all through the year. When springtime comes, she's knee-deep in moon shavings, so she sets out for her favorite tree, the black locust, and hangs her moon shavings from its boughs, which is why, come May, you'll find the locust adorned with pale moons of petal, clustered in crescents. *The Old Farmer's Almanac*, something of a back-up Yankee bible to generations of skywatchers and continent-crossing pioneers, was rife with lunar legend, beginning with the litany of each month's full-moon names, a poetic read of the earth's rumblings from February's Snow Moon to June's Strawberry Moon and onto December's Long Night Moon. Among the moon-tied agrarian wisdoms: during waxing moon (from new moon to full), sow seeds of crops bearing above-ground fruits, and plant the seeds of root crops on waning-moon days, a teaching that taps into the moon's gravitational pull, believed to affect moisture in soil as well as the ocean's tides.

The etiology of moonlight, that silvering that drapes half the globe at a time, is a story of reflectivity, which might hold some inkling of illumination for those who think in theological terms, as it allows us to see, in the hard numbers of science, how radiance works. It reminds: we need only turn to our center-stage sun—the divine one, the original light I know as my God—to absorb a trace of the holiest aura, to bask in our own meant-to-be radiance. In the case of the moon, it goes something like this: The first sparks of light shoot from the sun at a rate close to 186,000 miles per second, soaring through space for eight minutes, or ninety-three million miles, where some fraction of photons then bounce off the lunar landscape for a sprint of another 1.3 seconds, or 240,000 miles, piercing through the layers of earth's atmosphere, and finally raining down—celestial light show—on the world out our windows. That it gets to us at all, that our nighttime is anything less than sheer blackout, is nothing short of astronomical stunner. No wonder we've been agog at the moon for all time.

And what of the soulful side of the moon? It seems to be up there, hanging by its invisible thread in the diorama of sky, provoking perpetual proverbial ponderings. There's its ceaseless shape-shifting, from new moon to full, and back again, that seems to pin to the blackboard an unending lesson in life after death; some call it the resurrection moon. Ancient Jews, so taken with this starting-all-over-again, originally ordained the new moon their Sabbath moon, and even now the new beginning, Rosh Hodesh, "head of the month," is marked as a minor festival. The early Talmudic scholar Rabbi Yochanan, in the third century, compared blessing the new moon in its appointed time to greeting God himself. It was taught, "If the Israelites were privileged to greet their father in heaven once a month, that would be enough for them." Until the fourth century, the spying of the new moon was serious business for Jews, whose whole calendar was and is ordered lunarly. A special court of seventy-one sages, called the Sanhedrin, would proclaim the new moon, but only after two witnesses came to them with news of the first sighting. Using a long torch on top of the Mount of Olives in Jerusalem, someone from the Sanhedrin would light a fire atop the hill, and thus word would spread from hilltop to hilltop and valleys below. Even now, a beautiful prayer, *Birkat Halevanah*, the blessing of the new moon, is said outdoors, under the heavens, following the first Shabbat after the new moon. As the prayer unfurls, the prayerful rise to their toes—or climb atop each other's shoulders—while gazing at the moon, reciting, in part, "And to the moon He said that it should renew itself as a crown of beauty for those He carried from the womb, as they are destined to be renewed like it, and to praise their Creator. . . . Blessed are You the Lord, Who renews the months." And then, under the light of that new wisp of moon, those praying turn one to another, with the words, *Shalom aleichem*, peace be with you. It's emphasized that the prayer is not praising the moon but the Creator—*borei*, *koneh*, *poel*, and *yotser*, four Hebrew synonyms for "creator." Both Torah (the Scripture) and Talmud (the teachings thereof) are stitched with moon-tied mention and mitzvot, or commandments; hardly surprising given that the Jews, like all early tribes, charted their ways by the timekeeping heavens. The Talmud decrees, "The other nations count by the sun, while Israel counts by the moon." For a people whose own history has had its phases of terrible darkness, the moon's promise of return and return is one that cannot be dimmed.

The Celts, another Indigenous people—defined as "entwined with a particular place," in this case permeated by their unforgiving slice of God's earth, amid the hard winds and battering seas of the North Atlantic—paid mind to the moon, as did so many ancient peoples. While Celtic men bared their heads to the sun, the women, especially, hailed the new moon as "the great lamp of grace," and at first sighting of any night's moon, bent at the knee—or curtseyed—in homage. Though the sun was regarded with awe, the moon was more of a celestial friend, a great love who guided the Celts on their night paths. Men and women both were keen to run to a knoll or a hilltop to be the first to spy the new moon, where they'd anoint its first sliver with blessing. One such benediction ends, "If to-night, O moon, thou hast found us in peaceful, happy rest, may thy laving lustre leave us seven times still more blest." Truth was, every measure of moon held a particular grace for the Celts, who welcomed the way it danced *with* the darkness, interlaced, rather than seeking to snuff out the beauties and the mysteries of the middle-night hours. "Holy be each thing which she illumines," prayed the Celts, who understood the poetry and potency of darkness, and never shied from it. A critical distinction in their blessed-be of the moon is the understanding that it's not the moonlight that makes holy whatever it falls upon, as J. Philip Newell makes clear, but that "in her light the holiness of each thing is more readily perceived." Oh, that we should always so see. Bring on the moon's holy glow.

The prayer power of the night lamp hasn't waned over time. Not long ago, essayist Fred Bahnson retraced Thomas Merton's late-in-life pilgrimage to the American West, stopping first at the majestic redwoods along the California coast. That's where the Trappist monk fifty years earlier had spent two weeks with the Cistercian nuns of a monastery tucked amid the cathedral of goliathan old-growth trees. In Bahnson's conversations with one of the holy women there—a Belgian nun named Sister Veronique, who'd spent a few long-ago days with Merton—she pointed to the moon as crucial to her own prayerful epiphany, after a long, arid chapter when prayer was a struggle. Her "dawning realization that God was always and everywhere present came most from watching the moon," Bahnson recounted. For three nights, a moon she knew to be full was nowhere to be seen, she'd told him, hiding somewhere in the clouds. But, "just because she couldn't see it didn't mean it wasn't there, exerting its gravitational pull on her and on every other thing on earth. So it is with God. Always there, exerting a pull on us, but not always felt."

That very dawning is one that echoes my own from moonless nights on the beach. When faith is the thing that comes to you when you kneel in the dark on the sand in the night, and the lone goose calls to you, tells you it's there up above. It's all there, all where it's meant to be. All of creation, and yes, too, Creator—*borei, koneh, poel,* or *yotser,* Blessed Creator.

A LITANY OF
ASTONISHMENTS

Earth's crammed with heaven,
And every common bush afire with God;
But only he who sees, takes off his shoes. . . .

—Elizabeth Barrett Browning, nineteenth-century English poet

ℰ The blooming of the English bluebell is intricately timed to make use of the short spell of springtime when the soil is warming but the canopy of trees hasn't yet fully filled in with leaves. It's at the precise intersection of warmth + sunlight that the silver-drop woodland beauty, bent like a shepherd's crook, unfurls in a cobalt carpet.

ℰ Each spring, as the trees leaf out and the birds' nests are filled, there's a simultaneous profusion of caterpillars—soft, moist caterpillars, best meant for young baby birds whose bellies are hungry. There's intricate choreography at play here, with birds' mating timed to sync with nesting, hatching, and emergence of caterpillars, the perfect fledgling baby food.

ℰ In the head of a caterpillar, there are 228 separate and distinct muscles.

ℰ Not to be outdone, the dragonfly boasts twenty-five thousand eyes in the clear bubble of its head. The poor things never get shut-eye, because those eyes can never close.

ℰ Something to consider next time you wield a trowel: in the top inch of forest loam, biologists found an average of 1,356 living creatures present in each square foot. That census includes 865 mites, 265 spring tails, twenty-two millipedes, nineteen adult beetles, and various numbers of twelve other forms.

ℰ Orbital truths: planet Earth orbits around the sun at 64,800 miles per hour; our solar system—once described "like a merry-go-round unhinged, [that] spins, bobs, and blinks"—is downright slo-mo in comparison, gliding a mere 43,200 miles per hour along a course east of Hercules.

ℰ There is a take-your-breath-away symmetry and science behind the repetition of patterns in creation, a set series of templates, found over and over again. A few examples: Natural patterns form as wind blows sand in the dunes of the Namib Desert. The crescent-shaped dunes and the ripples on their surfaces repeat wherever there are suitable conditions. Other patterns recurring in nature include symmetries, spirals, trees and fractals, flow and meanders (sinuous bends in a river are no accident), waves and dunes, bubbles and foam, tessellations (think honeycombs), cracks, and spots and stripes. Early Greek philosophers—among them, Plato, Pythagoras, and Empedocles—studied pattern assiduously, attempting to explain order in nature. A trove of mathematical algorithms and inviolable geometries undergird all of it. And truly, it's breathtaking. Sometimes, the patterns hold layers of meaning; for instance, patterns of the veiled chameleon, *Chamaeleo calyptratus*, provide camouflage and signal mood as well as breeding condition. Think: lizard as mood ring. Symmetry itself is a whole nother wonder, pervasive in all creation from sea lilies to snowflakes.

EPILOGUE:
LAMENTATIONS
FOR THE
BOOK OF NATURE

There are no unsacred places;
there are only sacred places
and desecrated places.

—Wendell Berry, American poet, environmentalist, and farmer

In the thick files of field notes I've kept over the years, recording the dramas of life around this old shingled house and its miscreant gardens, the folder that barely shoves back in the drawer is the one marked "Heartbreak." And not because the humans who dwell here are of particularly dramatic disposition. It's simply the truth of keeping close watch on the wilds, even the genus of wild that comes in a leafy little town where time can be told by the whir and the whistle of commuter trains, where Saturday morning stillness is shattered by the incessant whine of leaf blowers down the block. Heartbreak around here is of the natural sort, the baby bird spilled from the nest, the cold snap that casts the pall of death over what had been a spring-time's unfolding, or the honeybees whose hives have dwindled to an eerie, barely audible thrum. Of all the lessons that unfurl in my earthy plots, the ones of rising up from heartbreak are the ones most prolific. To keep close watch on the shiftings of heaven and earth is to know the sharp pang of brittle brokenness, and to slow-breathe the salve of picking up the pieces, slogging onward, finding breath once again.

There are lessons in ephemerality, the reminder that all this is fragile, and none of it guaranteed, a truth you inhale over and over as you step into the dawn and discover petal after just-opening petal flash-frozen and fallen in the cold of the night. There are lessons in mercy, too, the times when you've res-cued a tumbled-down fledgling, scooped him onto your palm, felt the weight-lessness, felt the tickle of his tiny bird feet, the elation when at last he up and fluttered away. And, certainly, there are lessons in resilience as the weather gods thrust their battery of cruelties and tricks to see if we topple or stand.

But I'd be a fool if I thought that was the worst of it. What's saddest is how little we notice at all, how defiantly, arrogantly, we take it for granted. The sobering spine-stiffening truth is that, as a people, we've abandoned our watch on this one holy earth, and the losses are dire: personal, political, and, in the end, always sacred.

Of course it's long been the case that to turn the pages of the Book of Nature is to come to know the elegy, the language of grief, of sorrow, of heart-piercing brokenness. The small-scale heartbreaks, the ones that fall from your trees, or land by your toes, they hurt plenty. But the ones on the global scale, they're grief squared, and squared again. Or they should be. And the alarm is sounding louder than ever. The echoes rise all around. When the forest burns, and the skies thicken with smoke. When the river runs murky, or worse. And the lake turns red from a toxic bloom. Be it tsu-nami or cyclone, Steinbeckian drought or hundred-year flood. Or a pan-demic that locks down the globe for all of two years, leaving a death count in millions. If anyone's watching—and I think someone is—they might be thinking we're close to the edge.

The balance, as ever, is delicate. More delicate, perhaps, than we some-times pretend. For every shaft of sunlight, there's a concomitant shadow. It's the law of nature. Of Ecclesiastes. The Japanese know it as *mono no aware*, lit-erally "the pathos of things," the deep sorrow of beauty lost, or beauty tinged with sadness. The Italians name it *tristesse*, a particular melancholy, or beau-tiful sadness, often when crushed by earth, sea, or sky. In Latin, it's *prae con-tritione spiritus mundi*, the brokenness of the world. You can barely walk in the woods without stumbling on something that shatters your heart, cuts deep under our skin. Can barely scroll through the news without absorbing the lat-est assault on this deeply wounded planet. It's a stab every time. And, harsh-est of all, the woundedness flows both ways. Sure, some of it strikes from the heavens, or rises up from the underground, unpredictable, inexplicable. But too much of it is caused by our own mortal sin, our sloth, our gluttonies, our lust without end. And the insidious sin of looking away.

"We no longer read the Book of Nature," writes theologian Thomas Berry in his call to attention, *The Great Work.* "We no longer coordinate our human celebrations with the great liturgies of the heavens. . . . We have silenced too many of those wonderful voices of the universe that spoke to us of the grand mysteries of existence."

We've fallen so far from where we began—the opening pages of that great holy book. We no longer speak the language of creation's sacred rites. "We do not know the secrets of stars," Linda Hogan, the Chickasaw Nation poet and novelist, laments. Nor, she adds, do we listen for the innermost secrets of trees. Nor remember that wind is a prophet. Nor trust in the circular infinity of rain. "We have forgotten that this land and every life-form is a piece of god, a divine community. . . . Without respect and reverence for it, there is an absence of holiness, of any God." It's a memory so ancient we've lost trace of it.

Indeed, we no longer hear the voices of the rivers, the mountains, or the sea—the murmurs of this holy earth. We barely hear the birds out our own back door. And, what with all the pinging and buzzing, who can hear the bellows of wind? Or the plops of the early morning's rainfall when it's rinsing the garden?

The litany of losses, when we read closely the elegies of those who've stalked the woods and perched on the riverbanks, is finely filigreed and often unnoticed. The intimacies no longer known of heaven and earth are these: we've lost the feel of a hot dry wind on our face, the smell of distant rain, the touch of a bird's sharp foot on our outstretched hand, writes Robert Macfarlane in *The Wild Places*, after climbing in the Cumbrian Mountains one moonlit night in the Lake District of northwest England. "There is something uncomplicatedly true in the sensation of laying hands upon sun-warmed rock, or watching a dense mutating flock of birds, or seeing snow fall irrefutably upon one's upturned palm," he mused, before falling asleep under the stars.

A generation earlier, when the loss of the buffalo was still in memory, Aldo Leopold grieved the loss of a particular prairie wildflower, the cutleaf *Silphium*, or compass plant, that had once "tickled the bellies of the buffalo," noting the cost of extinction of the chin-high stalk spangled with saucer-sized sunflower blooms: "with it will die the prairie epoch," he wrote. So, too, the loss of the passenger pigeon: "No living [person] will see again the onrushing phalanx of victorious birds . . . chasing the defeated winter from all the woods and prairies," wrote the chronicler of Wisconsin's Sand County. "We grieve only for what we know," he argued, insisting we commit to heart the abundance around us so that we can know and grieve its absence.

The poetries of all that's lost in inferno or drought or the hand of human destruction cannot be too subtly chiseled. Writing of a centuries-ago human-sparked inferno, when the Spanish conquistador Hernando Cortes incinerated the aviaries of Montezuma's Iztapalapa—thousands of birds: vermilion flycatchers, blue-throated hummingbirds, copper-tailed trogons, and on and on through the color wheel—the Chickasaw poet Hogan captured the invisible. Cortes's army, she wrote, "burned even the sound of wings and the white songs of egrets." Seeing the unseen is why poets belong in the ranks of the holy. They keep census on the ineffable, the closest I know to God's sainted notetakers.

What are we to learn from a manuscript—ignored, worn ragged over the ages—that leaves us wrought and, not uncommonly, weeping? And what's the toll when the loss isn't merely our own, but a wound that gouges this whole holy earth? And how vast the grief when the gouge tears at the binding of this one sacred text that's meant to immerse us, enfold us, in the very Oneness who created the heavens and the earth, and saw that it was good? After all, it was only a few pages into Genesis when, in exuberant exultation, unable to contain the blessedness, unwilling to stingily hoard it, God thought to drop into the garden a pair of gardeners to "till it and keep it." If, from the get-go, the whole idea was to indulge in reciprocal delight, a reverie and illumination of every dimension, then what are we losing when we barely read it anymore, or, worse, tear out whole pages?

It's so deep a loss, and so lasting a brokenness, an Australian ecophilosopher gave a name to it back in 2005: *solastalgia*, described as distress caused by environmental change. It's "the homesickness you feel when you're still at home," explains Glenn Albrecht, who coined the neologism. The world's oldest medical journal, the *Lancet*, in 2015 identified solastalgia as a growing threat to human health, and tagged on a warning that we're "mortgaging the health of future generations" by "unsustainably exploiting nature's resources" via a long list of ails: "climatic change, ocean acidification, land degradation, water scarcity, overexploitation of fisheries, and biodiversity loss," among the diagnoses. The wounds, personal and political, are real. And the sacred, perhaps the least talked about, might be the cruelest of all.

To fully grasp the spiritual wounds, we need some sense of the state of the planet here in the twenty-first century, particularly in the wake of an unparalleled pandemic that all but locked down the globe, leaving millions for dead and hundreds of millions suffering. Ours is a planet of scourges seeming to mount by the decade, with climate disasters bigger and wider and deeper and fiercer than ever before. In *Annus horribilis* 2020, the planet was ravaged by forest fires that turned to ashes the American West, made for the most toxic air on the globe, and collected a toll that will never be fully tallied. Arctic sea ice, now an endangered species, is melting precipitously, a mysterious "cold blob" swirling through the North Atlantic wreaking hell and high water. In 2020 alone, the United States was slammed with a record-setting twenty-two weather-and-or-climate-disaster events, each with losses exceeding $1 billion, according to the National Oceanic and Atmospheric Administration. These disasters, as federally tabulated, included one drought, thirteen severe storms, seven tropical cyclones, and one wildfire, a roster that reads like a dirge and barely grasps the devastations.

Besieged by the unending assault of the accumulating crises, compounded by the pandemic, environmental writer Christopher Solomon, in the *New York Times*, grasped the urgency: "We tear at the days immoderately, like animals, and we wolf them down, hoping to fill a hole we see yawning ahead. There's not much time."

Disregard for the planet is hardly novel. We've been burning it, bulldozing it, mucking it up since Eve grabbed the fruit from the tree. (Well, maybe the bulldozing comes a few chapters later.) The point is: polluting the globe is an old, old problem. Even the ancient Romans worried about "heavy heavens," the haze in the air from all their cooking fires; Horace, the poet, fumed about those thousands of wood-burning fires, and bewailed old Rome's smoke-begrimed marble temples. By the 1600s, Londoners were choking on their coal-powered metropolis, and "the smoke of London" was a named—and nettlesome—entity, a way of life ingrained even in the literature that rose from the burg on the Thames. Charles Dickens, for instance, in the opening lines of *Bleak House*, permeated the page with it: "Smoke lowering down from chimney-pots, making a soft black drizzle, with flakes of soot in it as big as full-grown snow-flakes— gone into mourning, one might imagine, for the death of the sun." And that was 1852. In America, where the pioneer creed was to conquer the wilderness, the mountaineer John Muir sought to snuff the smoke. He had his own Dickensian moment when, in his 1901 treatise *Our National Parks*, he complained of "these hot, dim, strenuous times." People, he said, were "choked with care like clocks full of dust, laboriously doing so much good." His prescription was not to clear the dust but rather to run from the broken cities, to head for the hills, forge into the wilds. And so it's an echo without end when ecophilosopher David Abram succinctly bemoans, "We seem, today, so estranged from the stars, so utterly cut off from the world of hawk and otter and stone."

Prophets, the ones who see through the smog, keep trying to point to what's being ground down to dust. And it's not only the planet. Nearly a century ago, Henry Beston, one of those prophets, sitting in his farmhouse in Maine, worried about the state of the natural world, with the postindustrial era and the digital revolution still off in the unimaginable distance. "It is only when we are aware of the earth and of the earth as poetry that we truly live," he wrote, presciently. "Ages and people which sever the earth from the poetic spirit, or do not care, or stop their ears with knowledge as with dust, find their veins grown hollow and their hearts an emptiness echoing to questioning." He worried about the alienation from nature, "unexampled in history," whittling away throughout the entire nineteenth century, when the farming population was dwindling. He saw the farms, far from factory smoke, as "the living link with the mystery of earthly existence, with the poetry and beauty of our human heritage, with what may be possible and what impossible, with life, with death."

If we're no longer hoeing the rows, Beston implored, at least let us hold onto ancient wisdoms. His concern is all the more crucial today, when we're more severed than ever from this holy earth. Those wisdoms, the ones at risk of ebbing away, cannot be imparted if we're plunked before screens and tethered to digital cords; they're learned only through lives where it's not simply an accident—or a weekend's rustic-chic getaway—to rub up against the elements. To get soaked in a gusher. Or stung with a nettle. To wake up with the dawn, not some dagnabbed digital alarm. To fall asleep not with Ambien, but by counting the stars.

Even before the pace-braking coronavirus pandemic, Paul Kingsnorth, a poet, novelist, and "recovering environmentalist" living in rural Ireland, put his finger on the same diagnosis as Beston: there's a spiritual void, especially when it comes to the landscape. We're not seeing the sacred; we've stripped out the liminal space where the holy resides. "We've convinced ourselves that everything that matters can be measured," begins Kingsnorth, who came to believe the politics of activism obscured what's truly at stake. "The way that we react to a beautiful forest, or a sunset on a mountain, or a whale breaching in the ocean . . . it stirs something in you. . . . It's very real, but because you can't put it into words or measure it, we treat it as if it isn't real." Without a sense of the holiness, otherness, wonder, and beauty in all of creation, he adds, "you haven't got anything. You've lost one of the most central parts of being human."

Kingsnorth's point, and Beston's before him, and the point of all those raising a song of lamentation, is the one that most unsettles me. In a world that's assaulted and numbed, it's not exactly going out on a limb to say that, more than ever, we need the sacred. And the Book of Nature is the one sure text that, until now, has never run out of ways to draw us in to the heartbeat of God. To find ourselves caught by surprise. Uncertain of what just snatched our breath away, but certain it was something bigger and grander and wilder than we'll ever be.

Because this is a world that likes to haul out its measuring sticks and put numbers to things, here's the cost of planetary disregard and degradation in measurable terms, using only a few plot points from recent natural history.

Birds, first; birds falling from the sky, specifically: For migrating birds— some not much heavier than a leaf, some the size of a small chicken—Chicago, the city I call my own, is a sky-scraping, crazy-making obstacle of light and glass and building block thrown in the path of their flyway, that airspace that stretches from the northern boreal forests of Canada down to the pristine rain forests of Peru. Thousands of songbirds die each migration as they try to navigate the city's night sky, mistaking kilowatts for stars. It's particularly deadly on overcast nights when low-slung clouds occlude celestial stars and push the birds to lower altitudes. And at the dawn it only seems to get worse, with lobbies lit up like overzealous Christmas tree lots, and tired, thirsty, hungry flocks banging into glass they can't see, let alone comprehend. Over a span of the last four decades, researchers who comb the downtown Chicago sidewalks in the early dawn during spring and fall migrations scooped up and counted 70,716 birds that fell to their death after crashing into steel-and-glass towers, making the nation's third-largest city no. 1 when it comes to bird-collision deaths. Annually, the Cornell Lab of Ornithology puts the national count for bird-collision deaths at six hundred million, a deadly swath that stretches coast to coast.

Burning forests: Wildfires torched more than four million acres in California in the epic infernos of 2020 and predicted a grim future of bigger and hotter and higher fires ahead. Years of drought and bark-beetle infestations made a tinderbox of the Western landscape, ready to go up in flames. And it did. Among the toll, some of the Pacific Coast's oldest and most majestic of trees. In the Sierra Nevada, amid ancient groves of giant sequoias, trees as old as the Bible, nearly two-thirds of the roughly 48,000 acres of sequoias have burned since 2015; the toll in the last five years alone is double what had burned in the previous century. In the Mojave National Preserve, one of the largest remaining stands of the otherworldly Joshua tree, a single blaze, the Dome Fire, killed 1.3 million trees in two days, leaving behind an ash-strewn moonscape of skeletal, collapsing Joshuas. And, perhaps the holy of sylvan holies, the old-growth redwoods, the tallest on earth, where fires swept through 97 percent of the redwood forests on the northern California coast in 2020, scorching the 4,400 acres of old-growth redwoods that have towered for thousands of years. Despite char two hundred feet up the trunk, at least some of the redwood giants refused to die, with bits of green spied near the tops. The trees are in a fight for their lives.

Even alpine wildflowers are in the crosshairs: The intricacies and complexities of the cosmos play out on the mountainside in a choreography of snow and wildflower and honeybee. It's not a happy dance. Those who keep close watch on the slopes, scientists and evolutionary botanists, have been recording the cascade of ill effect, and it goes like this: Mountain snows are the blanket for the understory of wildflower as it rises in the early spring. When the snows melt too soon, the buds of the flowers are prone to frostbite. When the flowers thin or wither or die, the bees have no pollen, the bears and the birds and the wild things have too little to eat, and the seeds of the flower don't scatter. The French-knotted carpet of alpine blossom, once thought indelible, fixed to the mountain, is fading. In the last forty years, the snows have melted about two weeks earlier than ever before, a melt that's changing the mountainside.

Can you even begin to imagine the *un*measurable losses in that short litany? Songbirds felled in midflight, a flight they've been following for millennia? Old-growth groves and their vast woodland ecosystems where the mysteries and majesties of the forest have played out in the dance of the sacred for as long as there's been sunlight and soil and rain? The delicate embroidery of the mountainside, where wind and seed, bear and bee, all partake of creation and re-creation, a wheel of holy alchemy that's only now beginning to sputter?

There's a Siberian myth that when you close the smoke hole in a reindeer-hide tent—the orifice opening up to the sky—God can't see in anymore. You've clamped off the throughway to the divine, to the heavens and clouds and stars in the sky. When you close the smoke hole, according to the myth, you go mad in the whirl of unending toxic vapors. Sometimes I think maybe the world needs to open the smoke hole.

And how and where do we begin, in a world still shaken by the pandemic siege, and the unprecedented trials sure to come between the time I write this sentence and you read it? What on God's earth might bring us back to our holiest senses?

Remember heaven, is the prescriptive of the Walden woodsman, Henry David Thoreau, who lamented in 1846 that we, in our modernities, "have settled down on earth and forgotten heaven." It's a wisdom, he preached, that comes not through words on a page, but in the language of all those things—the woods, the birds, the turning of seasons—that speak without metaphor. The things that simply *are*. Those things that rustle and flutter and sing to us. It's why, in Thoreau's first summer at Walden, he hoisted a hoe and not a book. In hoeing the beans, the Transcendentalist immersed himself in "the bloom of the present moment," teaching himself "the discipline of looking always at what is to be seen." It's the spiritual practice of the ages, the practice of paying exquisite attention.

The cost of not practicing it, writes Sufi teacher Llewellyn Vaughan-Lee, is to live a "ghost's life," a life as that of the rootless exile, clinging to weeds and trees. The antidote he prescribes, as with Thoreau, is to indulge in whole-body attentiveness, a sensory aliveness: to run fingers against the bark and the leaves of a tree, to catch sight of the wild geese arrowing the autumn sky. "Life's wholeness is all around us," he teaches, "in every dawn chorus, every flower turning towards the sun. And yet our contemporary consciousness seems so fragmented."

How do we unfragment that consciousness, weave our tattered threads into a whole? Abram, the ecophilosopher, is not alone in pointing to the pandemic, ironically, as kickstarting the process: "It takes time and it takes slowing down, and the kind of slowing down that the pandemic has forced upon us, to become aware of one's breath, for instance." The very breath in our lungs, he points out, is one of those threads that's weaving us into the whole. It's infused with oxygen exhaled from the trees and the woods and the forest. All the planet is perpetually breathing as one, round and round we all breathe. It's time we notice. And the months and months of being tethered to wherever we called home, Abram writes, offered "a chance to actually apprentice ourselves to the weirdness of our particular locale." To learn by heart the birdsong and the swirl of the bark on the trees that breathe in our own backyards.

One imperative, no matter where or when, is accepting our vulnerability and fragility, and that of the world as well. If we're not palpably aware that none of this is forever—not our own breath after breath, not the gossamer web that holds all the world enlaced in delicate balance—then we can't begin to lift the veil, to see what's beyond, to absorb all of creation with necessary awe. Nor grasp all that we'll otherwise miss. We've only the glimpse of the now. The snowflakes are melting, the seashores are shrinking, the call of the wild is fading.

It's ours to love, this Book of Nature offering page after page to pore over—this book with its infinite lessons, its thousand embraces. If only we put down our distractions and behold it—all of it, any of it.

And if we don't? If we turn away from the God who wrote the whole of this, who waits to bump up against us, to delight, to mystify, to astonish, to catch us midbreath, deep in the shadowy woods or the still of the night, in the high notes of birdsong at dawn or the forlorn echo of the owls in the dusk? If we cut ourselves off from this God of infinite and intimate encounter, how in the world will we ever join in the cosmic dance?

This God of creation, I'm thinking, is a God who wants to be known not simply in words on a page, but in the butterfly couplet shimmering across a lazy afternoon, the lonely cry of the unseen geese's night crossing, the frost ferns on the windowpanes.

One of the images that carries me forward, that drops me to my knees, truth be told, is this: in his modern-day poetries of ancient mystics, in a book titled *Love Poems from God*, Daniel Ladinsky draws from Teresa of Avila's writings to illuminate her image of God who "kneels over this earth like a divine medic," and whose love "thaws the holy in us." I home in on the word *holy*, an Old English word, originally *hālig*, which also meant whole, as in not separated, not divided or broken. Maybe it's meant for us to see the earth not as a collection of separate parts, of brokenness—either-or commodities, each with a pricetag, to be protected or exploited—but as one sacred inseparable whole.

It is the very wholeness, that holiness, that draws me out from under my bedsheets in the half-light of the dawn. It is, perhaps, my old nurse's heart that compels me to step under heaven's dome, to drop to my knees, and to kneel over this holy wounded earth, beside the divine medic, to offer those few tools I've honed. Eyes to see—the subtlest stirrings in the leaves, the currents, and the clouds. Ears to hear—creation's song whispered near and in the distance. Heart and soul to absorb it all, and, in return, to reflect it heaven's way—in my tenderness, my awe, and my prayer without end.

As I pore over the Book of Nature, from first to last, I'll not forget that in the making of the whole of this, in the chiseling of the stars, and the stitching of the meadow, in unfurling the seas and pouring every river, in entwining every vine and sculpting every canyon, the God who created this, the Divine Artificer, looked down upon his work and "saw everything that he had made, and indeed, it was very good."

I can't bear to look away. Can't imagine how hollow this brokenness must be for the one who wants nothing more than to open the book, spread it before us, and catch us out in the wild, poring over each page.

This day will not come again.

—Thomas Merton, twentieth-century Trappist monk and author

A BOOKSHELF
OF WONDER

The weaving and writing of this book has been, as much as anything, an adventure in deep reading across centuries and subjects. I have shimmied onto the shoulders of pilgrims and poets, naturalists and monastics, from all traditions and teachings. From the rows and stacks of books and papers that now rim the room where I write, here are the dozen or so titles or authors whose works most profoundly and broadly informed and inspired the making of this book. Because I've plumbed twelve pages from the Book of Nature, each of which magnifies a particular subject, and thus draws on the works of particular authors, I bring your attention to a few especially wondrous titles and writers for those, each under its own subheading. Beyond the bulging bookshelves, I've another deep well: I've long been a keeper of a commonplace book, an old-fashioned compendium of words that dizzy me, poetries that set me soaring, and bits of esoterica and wonderment that charm me to no end. Because I was and ever will be a journalist by heart, I source those bits every time, and it was that lifelong collection into which I dipped joyfully in writing these chapters and essays. I'm an ardent proponent of what I call the Russian-doll method of reading, one writerly work opening into another, following citations and mentions from title to title. What follows is the record to-date; to be continued. I bring infinite gratitude to all assembled here, and all yet to come.

***

If you're keen to read prose that's sumptuously poetic as it illuminates the natural world, prose that shimmers at the edge of the sacred without ever aligning itself with any definable deity, or in some cases even conceding belief, these are perpetual keepers:

Pilgrim at Tinker Creek, by Annie Dillard.

This book, a 1974 Pulitzer Prize–winning nonfiction narrative, is my North Star. Dillard takes us into the woods and along the creek behind her then-home (you'd never guess it was a quotidian brick ranch house, complete with picture window, and the creek an unassuming stream meandering through suburbia) in the Blue Ridge Mountains outside Roanoke, Virginia. She makes us see the unseen, and while she writes of giant water bugs and shooting stars, minnows and maple keys, she calls *Pilgrim* not a nature book but a "book of theology." No less than Eudora Welty, in an early review, wrote that "the book is a form of meditation, written with headlong urgency, about *seeing*." Deeply influenced by Henry David Thoreau's *Walden*, Dillard's hours along the creek fill her notebook—and our imaginations—with dizzyingly lush field notes as she stalks, ultimately, for God.

The Best of Beston: A Selection from the Natural World of Henry Beston from Cape Cod to the St. Lawrence, by Henry Beston, edited and introduced by Elizabeth Coatsworth.

The Art of Seeing Things: Essays by John Burroughs, by John Burroughs, edited by Charlotte Zöe Walker.

Allow me to combine these two, both master teachers in a curriculum of seeing: Burroughs, a master of the eloquent essay, certainly in his collection *The Art of Seeing Things*; and Beston (*The Best of Beston* assembles the most beautiful passages from *Outermost House, Northern Farm*, and a lifetime of letters) still stands as one of American literature's most meticulous observers. Burroughs, a compatriot of Walt Whitman and John Muir, was no stranger to farm life or romps in the fields, fluent in birdsong and speckled trout, sap-letting and cow paths through snow, and thus earned his title as a literary naturalist. Burroughs's close-to-home approach, sticking to the Hudson River Valley and the Catskills he knew best, informed my knowing that I needn't trek far to behold nature's majesties.

The Star Thrower, by Loren Eiseley, introduction by W. H. Auden.

Eiseley, an anthropologist, naturalist, poet, and humanist, has been called "an heir of Thoreau and Emerson." With good reason. His probing meditations on the whole of the cosmos, taking in the sweep of natural history from the Big Bang onward, stand among the twentieth century's best. *Christian Century* once called attention to a study of Eiseley's work, writing, "The religious chord did not sound in him, but he vibrated to many of the concerns historically related to religion." In fact, in his autobiography, Eiseley stated, "I who profess no religion find the whole of my life a religious pilgrimage." To a reader of the Book of Nature, he is the surgeon peeling back the epidermis so we can behold the wonder of the workings within. Eiseley gathered this collection of his favorite writings shortly before his death in 1977.

Wildwood: A Journey through Trees, by Roger Deakin.
The Wild Places, by Robert Macfarlane.

Best read in tandem, or in breathless succession: traipsing the British Isles with this duo opens not only your eyes, but every literary piston tucked in your mind. The two well-trod writers shared not only a "paternal-filial friendship" (so described by Macfarlane in the wake of Deakin's sudden death in the summer of 2006) but a love of literature and of the wild, an intoxicated, impassioned love, one that had them both pinging around the countryside like mad molecular ions on the loose. While Macfarlane is sleeping on cliffs or deep in snowy woods, Deakin was poking around the sacred groves of Devon or crossing an Essex meadow at dusk to get to a rookery where, among other sonic astonishments, he listened for the whisper of wood pigeon wings. Together, theirs is a priceless tutorial: how to put into words the boundless wonder and marvel of the holiest wilds.

Living on the Wind: Across the Hemisphere with Migratory Birds, by Scott Weidensaul.

Though subject specific (the wondrous migrations of birds), *Living on the Wind* belongs on this short list of essential readings for anyone inclined to open the Book of Nature. That's because of Weidensaul's masterful capacity to translate complex scientific concepts and data into utterly poetic and picturable prose. A columnist for the *Philadelphia Inquirer* when he wrote this (trekking the globe to do so), Weidensaul trumpets a rare journalistic adroitness that, page after page, combines scientific sinew with literary finesse to churn out a tome already termed "a classic of natural history." Deservedly so.

***

If you're keen to absorb the theologies that imbue the idea of the Book of Nature, to connect dots between sacred text and millennia of scholarship, these theologians—a rabbi, two monks, and two ordained ministers (one a Celt who recently relinquished his ordination from the Church of Scotland, and the other a professor emeritus at a Jesuit college in middle America)—elucidate and illuminate:

The Great Conversation: Nature and the Care of the Soul, by Belden C. Lane.

Lane's breadth of knowledge and wisdom made me want to dial him up and enroll in his theology of nature courses; instead, I devoured his books, especially *The Great Conversation*. Lane, professor emeritus of theological studies, American religion, and the history of spirituality at Saint Louis University, as well as a man who freely admits to being in love with a hundred-year-old eastern cottonwood in an urban park across from his house, seems dead-set on saving not only the planet, but all of its people. He's a sojourner who seeks and finds the divine from the wolves of Yellowstone to the sandhill cranes of the Platte River Valley in central Nebraska. Lane pairs each of twelve wilderness expeditions with historical spiritual guides, interlacing biography with on-the-scene narrative, all of which buttress his central argument that, as a species, we humans have cut ourselves off from a life-saving conversation with all of creation. And we're doomed if we fail to alter our course.

Moral Grandeur and Spiritual Audacity: Essays, by Abraham Joshua Heschel, edited by Susannah Heschel.
The Sabbath: Its Meaning for Modern Man, also by Heschel, with introduction by Susannah Heschel.

I have spent so many hours with Heschel's writings, his words are inscribed on my heart. Beginning with the brilliance of the title, *Moral Grandeur and Spiritual Audacity*, the collected essays of the rabbi who fled Nazi Germany to become a Jewish savant of the twentieth century pulse with a piety and moral outrage that reshaped thinking in their time, and radiate still. *The Sabbath*, a slim and elegant volume, has aptly been described as "a masterpiece of religious thought," one that plumbs the holiness of time's most sacred hours. It was, for me, the door that first led me to the sacred that shimmers at the radiant core of Judaism, an ancient and blessed religion whose holy river now whirls around and through me.

Bread in the Wilderness, by Thomas Merton.
New Seeds of Contemplation, by Merton.
"Poetry, Symbolism and Typology" in *The Literary Essays of Thomas Merton*, of course by Merton.
Thoughts in Solitude, by Merton.

Merton, Trappist monk and prolific, best-selling twentieth-century author, built his cement-block hermitage in a silent corner of the woods surrounding the Abbey of Gethsemani in bucolic Kentucky, under a grove thick with pine trees. Need we know more? For Merton, the solitude and silence of God's unfettered creation were necessary to his contemplative life; every angle of sunlight, every storm convulsing the woods, it all was the prayer book from which Merton prayed. He led me deep into the Book of Nature and deep into meditations on stillness, especially in *New Seeds of Contemplation* and *Thoughts in Solitude*.

The Book of Creation: An Introduction to Celtic Spirituality, by J. Philip Newell.
Listening for the Heartbeat of God: A Celtic Spirituality, by Newell.
Sacred Earth, Sacred Soul: Celtic Wisdom for Reawakening to What Our Souls Know and Healing the World, by Newell.

I deep-dove into Celtic Christianity with writings across the millennia, from the fourth-century letters of Pelagius to the compendium of nearly-lost Gaelic prayer, *Carmina Gadelica*, to

Newell's more recent rekindlings of Celtic spirituality, especially *Sacred Earth, Sacred Soul*, from 2021. Newell, once the warden of Iona Abbey, an ancient and rebuilt relic in the Western Isles of Scotland, now resides in Edinburgh, where he runs his School of Earth and Soul. In *Sacred Earth*, he carries the reader across Celtic history, unfurling the stories of nine prophets who preached the Celtic way of seeing the sacred in whole of creation. My bookshelf is filled with Newell's Celtic prayers, poems, and psalters, all of which train my ear to listen for the heartbeat of God in all things under the sun and the moon, and beyond.

Music of Silence: A Sacred Journey through the Hours of the Day, by David Steindl-Rast, and Sharon Lebell, introduction by Kathleen Norris.

Steindl-Rast, a gentle-spirited Benedictine monk, counts among his worldwide flock believers and nonbelievers alike. By inviting each and all into the monastic practice of attending to the rhythms of sun and shadow, returning to prayer at eight fixed hours, from night watch to lauds to compline, this little book has anointed my nights and my days like no other. *Music of Silence*, with its beautiful imagery and its beckoning of angels, reframed my whole sense of time. Each turn of the prism, each season of the day, as Steindl-Rast terms the slow sweep of hourly time, brings its own encounter with mystery and quietest ecstasy.

***

If you're searching for writers whose fluency with field and flock, plain and pueblo, is ancestral, passed through the accumulated wisdoms of generations of story gatherers and storytellers, these are voices to commit to heart:

The Home Place: Memoirs of a Colored Man's Love Affair with Nature, by J. Drew Lanham.

Sparrow Envy: Field Guide to Birds and Lesser Beasts, also by Lanham.

Akin to the focus of his life's work, Lanham's poetries and prose take flight. Whether he's renaming birds in *Sparrow Envy,* releasing them from the bondage of "white-supremacist men with the self-serving penchant for naming things after themselves," or considering whether enslaved field workers toiling in the shadows of passing flocks might have looked skyward and imagined themselves unbound by "the weight of oppression," Lanham is a bracing and necessary poetic voice among bird-watching ranks. Mightily, he calls *Sparrow Envy* an "intensification of all that's brown and easily overlooked."

Black Nature: Four Centuries of African American Nature Poetry, edited by Camille T. Dungy.

This anthology, claimed to be the first such collection of nature writing by Black poets, gathers 180 poems from ninety-three poets, across four hundred years, a sweep of history from slavery, Reconstruction, the Harlem Renaissance, the Black Arts movement, clear through to the early twenty-first century. These are the poetics that rose, in part, from workers of the fields and herders of flocks, and though they defy pastoral conventions of Western poetry, they are every bit pastoral, describing moss and caves, rivers and hanging trees. In images not soon erased, these poems explore connection to, but also alienation from, the land. Seeping through many, a spiritual communion. Dungy has gathered us a trove.

Braiding Sweetgrass: Indigenous Wisdom, Scientific Knowledge, and the Teachings of Plants, by Robin Wall Kimmerer.

A botanist and member of the Citizen Potawatomi Nation, Kimmerer (winner of the John Burroughs Medal for outstanding nature writing) calls her collection of essays and meditations on the teachings of plants a "pharmacopoeia of healing stories." It's a journey through asters and goldenrods, strawberries and squash, algae and sweetgrass—as soulful as it is scientific. With Kimmerer as guide, we can't help but grasp earth's bedazzlements. And there begins our ache to heal this broken world.

Dwellings: A Spiritual History of the Living World, by Linda Hogan.

A brilliant collection of essays—seen through the wisdoms of Hogan's Chickasaw lens—*Dwellings* explores landscapes natural and interior, whether it's the language of corn or a sweat lodge healing ceremony, a "place grown intense and holy." From her first sentence, Hogan makes it easy to imagine we're seated at the foot of a wisdom keeper, one who lights ancient fires under star-stitched domes, and whose warmth and illuminations will carry us through till dawn breaks.

***

If pure poetry, with a double-shot of epiphany, is what you hunger for, *and* you're making me pick only one, it has to be this:

Long Life: Essays and Other Writings, by Mary Oliver.

I've long considered Oliver the patron saint and poet laureate of the woods, marsh, and saltwater tide. Her poetries—an oeuvre that counts nearly forty volumes—are shot through with epiphany, as is *Long Life*, a book of sumptuously poetic prose. The Pulitzer Prize-winning poet's sometimes ornate, sometimes subtle examinations of her Cape Cod surrounds, whether in stanza or paragraph, ring with earth praise, and play something akin to peekaboo with the presence of an often-unnamed holy Creator. Upon her death from lymphoma in 2019, the *New York Times* in her obituary wrote that her poems, "built of unadorned language and accessible imagery, have a pedagogical, almost homiletic quality." I'll take her sermons any old day.

***

If you've a taste for mind-bending philosophies swirled with fine prose, richly rooted in the natural world, populate your bookshelves with these:

The Spell of the Sensuous: Perception and Language in a More-Than-Human World, by David Abram.

Considered a classic of ecological philosophy, and one of the first books I read as I began to immerse myself in the scholars best equipped to guide me through the Book of Nature, Abram's *The Spell of the Sensuous* can be mind bending, and always intellectually bracing. It sets out as an inquiry of language, an examination of human interaction with the sensuality of the natural landscape, and argues toward Abram's simple premise that we are human "only in contact, and conviviality, with what is not human." Ours is an ages-old reciprocity with a many-voiced landscape, our every encounter with Thunder, Oak, or Dragonfly, he argues, informs our collective sensibility, defines who we are as species and individual. The color of sky, the rush of the waves, all of it shapes us. In other words, the whole of creation—and our engagement with it—is an imperative. Abram writes, "Without the oxygenating breath of the forests, without the clutch of gravity and the tumbled magic of river rapids, we have no distance from our technologies . . . no way to keep ourselves from turning into them."

Anything from *The Marginalian* (formerly *Brain Pickings*), by Maria Popova.

Popova, an unparalleled cultural critic, voracious reader, and sub-lime maker of sense, is my twice-weekly emailed dose of esoter-ica and wonder. Since 2006, formerly under what she terms "the unbearable name" of *Brain Pickings*, and now more elegantly *The Marginalian*, Popova has been gathering and dispatching online posts animated by her intellectual, spiritual, and poetic curiosi-ties. She's written that hers is a "search for meaning across liter-ature, science, art, philosophy, and the various other tendrils of human thought and feeling." And she claims that hers is private inquiry (now shared vastly publicly), irradiated by the ultimate question, "What *is* all this?" I'm perched at the edge of my seat, and I'm listening.

Walden and Other Writings, by Henry David Thoreau, edited and with introduction by Joseph Wood Krutch.
Walking, by Thoreau.

If there is a first apostle among woods wanderers, it has to be Tho-reau, and his most sacred text, indisputably, *Walden*, first published in 1854. Yet another title worth committing to heart is the one that traces his peripatetic tendencies, *Walking*, published in 1862. Both are necessary primers for igniting the cognitive powers that made Thoreau a master at navigating life, wilderness, and meaning, all in the space of a single (often long) sentence. Thoreau opened the door for us to imagine the same.

***

PAGES FROM THE BOOK OF NATURE

These are the works that most informed my meditations and meanderings on the twelve pages from the Book of Nature I chose to slide under my magnifying lens. (Complete references are included in the bibliography, each grouped accordingly.)

GARDEN

Loren Eiseley's *Star Thrower* charmed for a thousand reasons, but his classic essay "How Flowers Changed the World" changed everything; it is every bit as astonishing as promised. The late Roger Deakin's *Wildwood* belongs on a shelf all its own. Thor Hanson's *Triumph of Seeds*, and Robin Wall Kimmerer's *Braiding Sweetgrass*, are botanic wonders; Kimmerer's Potawatomi wisdom illuminates. Linda Hogan's *Dwellings*, especially her telling of the seeds of Hiroshima, is unforgettable; her Chickasaw lens and stockpile of story underscore timeless Sacred Earth wisdoms. John Hersey's unforgettable "Hiroshima" in the *New Yorker* stands as a masterpiece of narrative nonfiction.

WOODS

Trees and woods have attracted an especially prolific bookshelf: Henry David Thoreau would be the master, rivaled by Deakin's *Wildwood*, David George Haskell's *Songs of Trees*, Fiona Stafford's *Long, Long Life of Trees*, and Colin Tudge's *Secret Life of Trees*. The chance to reread Brother Lawrence's little gem, *The Practice of the Presence of God*, is always welcome. Richard Higgins's *Thoreau and the Language of Trees* is an excellent subject-specific lens into the woods of Walden Pond.

WATER'S EDGE

Mostly, sitting on the shore of Lake Michigan, a ten-minutes' walk from my house, was where I went to absorb water's wisdoms. Belden Lane's *Great Conversation*, as always, offered history and insight. Olivia Laing's *To the River* was pure delight, and Daniel Burnham's 1909 *Plan of Chicago* captured the sweep of Chicago's gem of a lake, and what it means to the pulse of the city.

EARTH'S TURNING

Henry Beston's eyeglass to the turning earth, especially from *Outermost House* and *Northern Farm*, captured beauties and wonders that escape most anyone else. Maria Popova here and elsewhere is one of contemporary culture's finest critics; I read her religiously.

BIRDS

Maybe it's just me, but the bird books on my shelves have grown to a voluminous flock. Especially wondrous are the words of Haskell, in "The Voices of Words and the Language of Belonging," from *Emergence Magazine*, and Scott Weidensaul's *Living on the Wind*. Aldo Leopold's *Sand County Almanac* is a classic for many, many reasons. Bernd Heinrich's *Homing Instinct* and *Nesting Season* are packed with science. Jennifer Ackerman's *Genius of Birds* amazes, and J. Drew Lanham's *Home Place* and *Sparrow Envy* enchant. Peggy Macnamara's *Architecture by Birds and Insects* astounds every time I open it.

GENTLE RAIN, THRASHING STORM

Melissa Harrison's *Rain* is a treasure, every page pure joy. John Muir's language of another age never ages. And Walt Whitman's *Specimen Days* belongs on the bookshelf of anyone who desires to see and sense the wonders of this holy world.

WIND

Who knew there was so much to know about the invisible element? The late Lyall Watson's *Heaven's Breath* is the place to begin, backed up by Jan DeBlieu's *Wind*, and Lane, again, with a chapter exploring the holy breath of the wind in *Great Conversation*. David Steindl-Rast's *Music of Silence* blessed with its commentary on breath and chant. Gavin Pretor-Pinney's *Cloud Collector's Handbook* is both eye-opening and instructive. And his wit is endless.

First Snow

Beston's winter scenes in *The Best of Beston*, nestled against Thoreau's snowy woods in *Walden* and his journals, could carry you through the longest coldest months. I'll read Robert Macfarlane anywhere, any season. And the science of snow, and its acoustic superpowers, drew me down quite a rabbit hole, deep into the Swiss Federal Institute of Snow and Avalanche Research SLF in Davos, Switzerland.

Dawn

Daybreak has ever enthralled. Steindl-Rast's *Music of Silence*, as well as the Celts—J. Philip Newell's *Celtic Benedictions*, and Alexander Carmichael's *Carmina Gadelica*—anoint the dawn with particular wonder. Thomas Merton's *Book of Hours*, as well as Rainer Maria Rilke's of the same name, echoed the wonder. Evelyn Underhill's *Worship* illuminated ancient Jewish practice.

Dusk

The particular holiness of dusk's liminal hour echoed in Macrina Wiederkehr's beautiful *Seven Sacred Pauses* and Steindl-Rast's *Music of Silence*. Deakin and Whitman put poetry to their keen attentions. And Patricia Lunetta's "The Visit," a poem I'd not have known except for Wiederkehr's citing of it, is one that will hold you long after you close the page.

Stars

H. A. Rey's *The Stars*, a book I pulled off my children's shelves, was eye-opening. Lane's *Great Conversation* masterfully wove history and insight. Again, Beston and Annie Dillard delight. The poetries of Pattiann Rogers's *Song of the World Becoming*, and Edward Hirsch's "In Spite of Everything, the Stars," in *Wild Gratitude*, make the night sky shimmer.

Moon

Most of my lunar observations seep in through watchkeeping. Fred Bahn-son, who went "on the road" with Merton (fifty years after the fact) for *Emergence Magazine*, shone a particular light. The Celts, as always, charm in *Carmina Gadelica*, and Newell's *The Book of Creation*. I can hardly look at the moon anymore without remembering, from Whitman's *Specimen Days and Collect*, his brilliant recounting of the long-ago *New-York Tribune*'s over-the-moon personifications.

LAMENTATIONS

Douglas E. Christie's *Blue Sapphire of the Mind* framed the ecospiritual urgen-cies, as did Thomas Berry's *Great Work*, David Abram's *Spell of the Sensuous*, and Lane's *Great Conversation*. Beston, in *Northern Farm* from *Best of Beston*, and Leopold, in *Sand County Almanac*, long ago raised their profound voices on the matter of what's at stake. I turned to newspapers, the *New York Times* and the *Chicago Tribune*, and federal agencies, the National Oceanic and Atmospheric Administration especially, for tracking the toll of the some of the latest natural disasters and climate devastations. *Emergence Maga-zine*, which trains its vision on the intersection of ecology and spirit, always enlightens, online, in print, and through voluminous webinars and courses.

BIBLIOGRAPHY

As long as this list is, it would be pages longer if I included every single title that's informed this book. All works cited are included here, along with readings that were otherwise essential or illuminating, even if not from which I quoted directly.

READING THE BOOK OF NATURE AND ON PAYING A PARTICULAR ATTENTION

Abram, David. *The Spell of the Sensuous: Perception and Language in a More-Than-Human World*. New York: Vintage Books, 2017. First published 1996.

Allchin, A. M., and Esther de Waal, eds. *Threshold of Light: Daily Readings from the Celtic Tradition*. London: Darton, Longman and Todd, 2019.

Aquinas, Thomas. *Thomas Aquinas: Selected Writings*. Edited by Ralph McInerny. London: Penguin Books, 1998.

Bashō, Matsuo. *The Narrow Road to the Deep North and Other Travel Sketches*. Translated and with introduction by Nobuyuki Yuasa. London: Penguin Books, 1966.

Berry, Thomas. *The Great Work: Our Way into the Future*. New York: Crown Publishing, 1999.

Buechner, Frederick. *The Remarkable Ordinary: How to Stop, Look, and Listen to Life*. Grand Rapids, MI: Zondervan, 2017.

Burroughs, John. *The Art of Seeing Things: Essays by John Burroughs.* Edited by Charlotte Zöe Walker. Syracuse, NY: Syracuse University Press, 2001.

Butcher, Carmen Acevedo. *St. Hildegard of Bingen: Doctor of the Church.* Brewster, MA: Paraclete Press, 2018.

Carmichael, Alexander. *Carmina Gadelica.* Vols. 1 and 2. Edinburgh, 1899.

Christie, Douglas E. *Blue Sapphire of the Mind: Notes for a Contemplative Ecology.* New York: Oxford University Press, 2013.

Chryssavgis, John. *In the Heart of the Desert: The Spirituality of the Desert Fathers and Mothers.* Rev. ed. Bloomington, IN: World Wisdom, 2008.

Comstock, Anna Botsford. *Handbook of Nature Study.* Ithaca, NY: Cornell University Press, 1986. First published 1939 by Comstock Publishing.

de Waal, Esther. *The Celtic Way of Prayer: The Recovery of the Religious Imagination.* New York: Doubleday, 1997.

Dillard, Annie. *Pilgrim at Tinker Creek.* New York: HarperCollins, 1998. First published 1974 by Harper's Magazine Press.

Doherty, Catherine de Hueck. *Poustinia: Encountering God in Silence, Solitude and Prayer.* Combermere, Ontario: Madonna House, 2012. First published 1993.

Dostoevsky, Fyodor. *The Brothers Karamazov.* New York: Vintage Books, 1950.

Dove, Rita. "Kentucky, 1833." *Paris Review,* Winter 1976. https://tinyurl.com/3ncd4dup.

Dreyer, Elizabeth A. *Accidental Theologians: Four Women Who Shaped Christianity.* Foreword by Joan Chittister. Cincinnati, OH: Franciscan Media, 2014.

Dungy, Camille T., ed. *Black Nature: Four Centuries of African American Nature Poetry.* Athens: University of Georgia Press, 2009.

Earle, Mary C. *Celtic Christian Spirituality: Essential Writings—Annotated & Explained.* Nashville: SkyLight Paths, 2011.

Eiseley, Loren. *The Star Thrower.* Introduction by W. H. Auden. New York: Times Books, 1978.

Emerson, Ralph Waldo. *The Selected Writings of Ralph Waldo Emerson.* Edited by Brooks Atkinson. New York: Random House, 1968. First published 1940 by Random House.

Eriugena, John Scotus, and Christopher Bamford. *The Voice of the Eagle: The Heart of Celtic Christianity*. Translated and with introduction by Christopher Bamford. Great Barrington, MA: Lindisfarne Books, 2000.

Fox, Matthew. *Original Blessing: A Primer in Creation Spirituality*. New York: Putnam, 2000.

———. *Passion for Creation: The Earth-Honoring Spirituality of Meister Eckhart*. Rochester, VT: Inner Traditions, 2000.

Green, Arthur. *Judaism for the World: Reflections on God, Life, and Love*. New Haven, CT: Yale University Press, 2020.

Guite, Malcolm. "Waiting on the Word." *The Trinity Forum*, December 18, 2020. https://tinyurl.com/kbxrhytc.

Harjo, Joy, Leanne Howe, and Jennifer Elise Foerster, eds. *When the Light of the World Was Subdued, Our Songs Came Through: A Norton Anthology of Native Nations Poetry*. New York: W. W. Norton, 2020.

Harrison, Peter. *The Bible, Protestantism, and the Rise of Natural Science*. New York: Cambridge University Press, 2001.

Heschel, Abraham Joshua. *Moral Grandeur and Spiritual Audacity: Essays*. Edited by Susannah Heschel. New York: Farrar, Straus and Giroux, 1996.

Higgins, Richard. *Thoreau and the Language of Trees*. Foreword by Robert D. Richardson. Oakland: University of California Press, 2017.

Hirshfield, Jane. *Nine Gates: Entering the Mind of Poetry*. New York: HarperCollins, 1997.

Hogan, Linda. *Dwellings: A Spiritual History of the Living World*. New York: W. W. Norton, 1995.

James, William. *The Varieties of Religious Experience: A Study in Human Nature*. London: Forgotten Books, 2015. First published 1902 by Longmans, Green, and Co.

Jeffers, Robinson. *The Wild God of the World: An Anthology of Robinson Jeffers*. Selected with an introduction by Albert Gelpi. Stanford, CA: Stanford University Press, 2003.

Johnson, Helene, and Verner D. Mitchell. *This Waiting for Love: Helene Johnson, Poet of the Harlem Renaissance*. Amherst: University of Massachusetts Press, 2000.

Julian of Norwich. *Julian of Norwich: Showings.* Translated by Edmund Colledge and James Walsh. New York: Paulist Press, 1978.

Laird, Martin. *Into the Silent Land: A Guide to the Christian Practice of Contemplation.* New York: Oxford University Press, 2006.

Lane, Belden C. *The Great Conversation: Nature and the Care of the Soul.* New York: Oxford University Press, 2019.

———. *Ravished by Beauty: The Surprising Legacy of Reformed Spirituality.* New York: Oxford University Press, 2011.

Leloup, Jean-Yves. *Being Still: Reflections on an Ancient Mystical Tradition.* New York: Paulist Press, 2003.

Leopold, Aldo. *A Sand County Almanac.* New York: Oxford University Press, 1966. First published 1949.

Li Po. *The Selected Poems of Li Po.* Translated by David Hinton. New York: New Directions, 1996.

Macfarlane, Robert. *The Wild Places.* London: Penguin Books, 2007.

Merton, Thomas. *Bread in the Wilderness.* New York: New Directions, 1953.

———. *New Seeds of Contemplation.* New York: New Directions, 1962.

———. "Poetry, Symbolism and Typology." In *The Literary Essays of Thomas Merton.* New York: New Directions, 1981.

———. *Thoughts in Solitude.* New York: Farrar, Straus and Giroux, 1999.

Newell, J. Philip. *The Book of Creation: An Introduction to Celtic Spirituality.* New York: Paulist Press, 1999.

———. *Listening for the Heartbeat of God: A Celtic Spirituality.* New York: Paulist Press, 1997.

———. *Sacred Earth, Sacred Soul: Celtic Wisdom for Reawakening to What Our Souls Know and Healing the World.* New York: HarperOne, 2021.

O'Donoghue, Noel Dermot. *The Mountain behind the Mountain: Aspects of the Celtic Tradition.* Edinburgh: T&T Clark, 1993.

Oliver, Mary. *Long Life: Essays and Other Writings.* Cambridge, MA: Da Capo Press, 2004.

———. *Our World.* Boston: Beacon Press, 2009.

Paz, Octavio. *The Bow and the Lyre: The Poem, The Poetic Revelation, Poetry and History.* Translated by Ruth L. C. Simms. Austin: University of Texas Press, 1991.

Rilke, Rainer Maria. *Rilke's Book of Hours: Love Poems to God.* Translated by Anita Barrows and Joanna Macy. New York: Riverhead Books, 2005.

Swartz, Daniel. "Israel Environment and Nature: A Brief History of Nature in Jewish Texts." Jewish Virtual Library. Accessed March 5, 2022. https://tinyurl.com/2p8nx736.

Teilhard de Chardin, Pierre. *The Divine Milieu.* New York: Harper & Row, 1960.

Thomas, R. S. "Perspectives." In *Collected Poems 1945–1990.* London: Phoenix Poetry, 2000.

Thoreau, Henry David. *Walden and Other Writings.* Edited and with introduction by Joseph Wood Krutch. New York: Bantam Books, 1982. First published 1854.

———. *Walking.* Bedford, MA: Applewood Books, 1988. First published 1862.

Underhill, Evelyn. *Evelyn Underhill: Essential Writings.* Selected and with an introduction by Emilie Griffin. Maryknoll, NY: Orbis Books, 2003.

———. *Worship.* Guildford, Surrey, UK: Eagle, 1991. First published 1936 by James Nisbet and Company.

Ward, Benedicta. *The Wisdom of the Desert Fathers: The Apophthegmata Patrum (the Anonymous Series).* Oxford: S. L. G. Press, 1975.

The Way of a Pilgrim. Translated by R. M. French. New York: HarperOne, 2010. First published 1954 by Harper.

White, Kenneth. *Handbook for the Diamond Country: Collected Short Poems 1960-1990.* Edinburgh: Mainstream Publishing, 1990.

Williams, Terry Tempest. *The Hour of Land: A Personal Topography of America's National Parks.* New York: Farrar, Straus and Giroux, 2016.

———. *Refuge: An Unnatural History of Family and Place.* New York: Vintage Books, 2018. First published 1991 by Pantheon Books.

Garden

Bahnson, Fred. *Soil and Sacrament: A Spiritual Memoir of Food and Faith.* New York: Simon & Schuster, 2013.

Day, Dorothy. *Thérèse.* Foreword by Robert Ellsberg. Notre Dame, IN: Ave Maria Press, 2016.

Deakin, Roger. *Wildwood: A Journey through Trees*. New York: Free Press, 2007.

de Waal, Esther. *The Celtic Way of Prayer: The Recovery of the Religious Imagination*. New York: Doubleday, 1997.

Eiseley, Loren. *The Star Thrower*. Introduction by W. H. Auden. New York: Times Books, 1978.

Hanson, Thor. *The Triumph of Seeds: How Grains, Nuts, Kernels, Pulses, and Pips Conquered the Plant Kingdom and Shaped Human History*. New York: Basic Books, 2015.

Hersey, John. "Hiroshima." *New Yorker*, August 31, 1946. https://tinyurl.com/57acyz7v.

———. "Hiroshima: The Aftermath." *New Yorker*, July 8, 1985. https://tinyurl.com/2p9ez67w.

Hogan, Linda. *Dwellings: A Spiritual History of the Living World*. New York: W. W. Norton, 1995.

Kimmerer, Robin Wall. *Braiding Sweetgrass: Indigenous Wisdom, Scientific Knowledge, and the Teachings of Plants*. Minneapolis: Milkweed Editions, 2013.

Merton, Thomas. *New Seeds of Contemplation*. New York: New Directions, 1962.

Steindl-Rast, David, and Sharon Lebell. *Music of Silence: A Sacred Journey through the Hours of the Day*. Introduction by Kathleen Norris. Berkeley, CA: Ulysses Press, 2002.

Thérèse of Lisieux. *Story of a Soul: The Autobiography of St. Thérèse of Lisieux*. Translated by John Clarke. Washington, DC: ICS Publications, 1996.

Woods

Deakin, Roger. *Wildwood: A Journey through Trees*. New York: Free Press, 2007.

Haskell, David George. *The Songs of Trees: Stories from Nature's Great Connectors*. New York: Viking, 2017.

Hesse, Hermann. *Wandering: Notes and Sketches*. Translated by James Wright. New York: Farrar, Straus and Giroux, 1972.

Higgins, Richard. *Thoreau and the Language of Trees*. Foreword by Robert D. Richardson. Oakland: University of California Press, 2017.

Hill, Libby. "North Shore Channel." In *The Chicago River: A Natural and Unnatural History.* Chicago: Lake Claremont Press, 2000.

Kimmerer, Robin Wall. "Skywoman Falling." *Emergence Magazine*, November 5, 2020. https://tinyurl.com/s9b5dyhn.

Lawrence, Brother. *The Practice of the Presence of God, with Spiritual Maxims.* Grand Rapids, MI: Spire Books, 1967.

Logan, William Bryant. *Oak: The Frame of Civilization.* New York: W. W. Norton, 2005.

Miyazaki, Yoshifumi. *Shinrin Yoku: The Japanese Art of Forest Bathing.* Portland, OR: Timber Press, 2018.

Oppenheimer, J. Robert. *Uncommon Sense.* Cambridge, MA: Birkhäuser Boston, 2013.

Otto, Rudolf. *The Idea of the Holy.* Translated by John W. Harvey. London: Oxford University Press, 1936.

Plato. *Meno.* Translated by Benjamin Jowett. The Internet Classics Archive. https://tinyurl.com/yh39fmf5.

———. *Meno.* Translated by G. M. A. Grube. 2nd ed. Indianapolis: Hackett Publishing, 1976.

Solnit, Rebecca. *A Field Guide to Getting Lost.* New York: Viking Penguin, 2005.

Stafford, Fiona. *The Long, Long Life of Trees.* New Haven, CT: Yale University Press, 2016.

Tanner, Helen Hornbeck, and Miklos Pinther. *Atlas of Great Lakes Indian History.* Norman: University of Oklahoma Press, 1987.

Thoreau, Henry David. *Walden and Other Writings.* Edited and with introduction by Joseph Wood Krutch. New York: Bantam Books, 1982. First published 1854.

———. *The Writings of Henry David Thoreau.* Boston: Houghton Mifflin, 1906.

Tudge, Colin. *The Secret Life of Trees: How They Live and Why They Matter.* London: Penguin Books, 2006.

Wohlleben, Peter. *The Hidden Life of Trees: What They Feel, How They Communicate—Discoveries from a Secret World.* Translated by Jane Billinghurst. Vancouver, BC: Greystone Books, 2016.

Water's Edge

Burnham, Daniel H., and Edwin H. Bennett. *Plan of Chicago*. Edited by Charles Moore. New York: Princeton Architectural Press, 1993. First published 1909 by the Commercial Club.

Laing, Olivia. *To the River: A Journey beneath the Surface*. Edinburgh: Canongate Books, 2011.

Lane, Belden C. *The Great Conversation: Nature and the Care of the Soul*. New York: Oxford University Press, 2019.

Earth's Turning

Beston, Henry. *The Best of Beston: A Selection from the Natural World of Henry Beston from Cape Cod to the St. Lawrence*. Edited and introduced by Elizabeth Coatsworth. Jaffrey, NH: Nonpareil Books, 2000.

Eckhart, Meister. *Sermons and Treatises*. Vol. 1. Translated and edited by M. O'C. Walshe. Longmead, Shaftesbury, UK: Element Books, 1987.

Galvin, James. *The Meadow*. New York: Henry Holt, 1992.

Haskell, David George. *The Songs of Trees: Stories from Nature's Great Connectors*. New York: Viking, 2017.

Iyer, Pico. *Autumn Light: Season of Fire and Farewell*. London: Bloomsbury Publishing, 2019.

Popova, Maria. "A Beginning, Not a Decline: Colette on the Splendor of Autumn and the Autumn of Life." *The Marginalian*, September 22, 2016. https://tinyurl.com/5bztxup.

Woodruff, Sue. *Meditations with Mechtild of Magdeburg*. Santa Fe: Bear & Company, 1982.

Birds

Ackerman, Jennifer. *The Genius of Birds*. New York: Penguin Books, 2017.

Haskell, David G. "The Voices of Birds and the Language of Belonging." *Emergence Magazine*, May 26, 2019. https://tinyurl.com/2p8ur33d.

Heinrich, Bernd. *The Homing Instinct: Meaning and Mystery in Animal Migration*. New York: Houghton Mifflin Harcourt, 2014.

———. *The Nesting Season: Cuckoos, Cuckolds, and the Invention of Monogamy.* Cambridge, MA: Belknap Press, 2010.

Lanham, J. Drew. "Forever Gone." *Orion Magazine*, Spring 2018. https://tinyurl.com/4k5kxu7f.

———. *The Home Place: Memoirs of a Colored Man's Love Affair with Nature.* Minneapolis: Milkweed Editions, 2016.

———. *Sparrow Envy: Field Guide to Birds and Lesser Beasts.* Spartanburg, SC: Hub City Press, 2021.

Leopold, Aldo. *A Sand County Almanac.* New York: Oxford University Press, 1966. First published 1949.

Macnamara, Peggy. *Architecture by Birds and Insects.* Chicago: University of Chicago Press, 2008.

Neruda, Pablo. *Pablo Neruda, Selected Poems: A Bilingual Edition.* Edited and with a foreword by Nathaniel Tarn. Introduction by Alastair Reid. Translated by Anthony Kerrigan, W. S. Merwin, Alastair Reid, and Nathaniel Tarn. Boston: Houghton Mifflin, 1990.

Weidensaul, Scott. *Living on the Wind: Across the Hemisphere with Migratory Birds.* New York: North Point Press, 1999.

Williams, Terry Tempest. *Refuge: An Unnatural History of Family and Place.* New York: Vintage Books, 2018. First published 1991 by Pantheon Books.

Gentle Rain, Thrashing Storm

Beston, Henry. *The Best of Beston: A Selection from the Natural World of Henry Beston from Cape Cod to the St. Lawrence.* Edited and introduced by Elizabeth Coatsworth. Jaffrey, NH: Nonpareil Books, 2000.

Harrison, Melissa. *Rain: Four Walks in English Weather.* London: Faber & Faber, 2016.

Jackson, Kenneth Hurlstone, trans. "The Hermit's Hut." In *A Celtic Miscellany: Translations from the Celtic Literatures.* London: Penguin Books, 1971. First published 1951 by Routledge & Kegan Paul.

Livio, Mario. "Mario Livio—Mathematics, Mystery, and the Universe." By Krista Tippett. *On Being Project*, March 11, 2022. https://tinyurl.com/mr2v6ckx.

Muir, John. *John of the Mountains: The Unpublished Journals of John Muir.* Madison: University of Wisconsin Press, 1966. First published 1938 by Houghton Mifflin.

————. *The Writings of John Muir: Our National Parks.* Boston: Houghton Mifflin, 1917.

Newell, J. Philip. *The Book of Creation: An Introduction to Celtic Spirituality.* New York: Paulist Press, 1999.

Swift, Jonathan. "A Letter of Advice to a Young Poet." In *English Essays: Sidney to Macaulay.* Vol. 27. The Harvard Classics. New York: P. F. Collier & Son, 1909–14. https://tinyurl.com/27au6f2j.

Whitman, Walt. *Specimen Days and Collect.* New York: Dover Publications, 1995. First published 1883 in Glasgow by Wilson & McCormick.

Wind

Abram, David. *The Spell of the Sensuous: Perception and Language in a More-Than-Human World.* New York: Vintage Books, 2017. First published 1996.

DeBlieu, Jan. *Wind: How the Flow of Air Has Shaped Life, Myth, and the Land.* New York: Houghton Mifflin, 1998.

Homer. *The Odyssey.* Translated by Robert Fagles. Introduction by Bernard Knox. New York: Penguin Group, 1997.

Lane, Belden C. *The Great Conversation: Nature and the Care of the Soul.* New York: Oxford University Press, 2019.

Pretor-Pinney, Gavin. *The Cloud Collector's Handbook.* San Francisco: Chronicle Books, 2011.

Steindl-Rast, David, and Sharon Lebell. *Music of Silence: A Sacred Journey through the Hours of the Day.* Introduction by Kathleen Norris. Berkeley, CA: Ulysses Press, 2002.

Tanakh: The Holy Scriptures. Philadelphia: Jewish Publication Society, 1985.

Thoreau, Henry David. *Walden and Other Writings.* Edited and with introduction by Joseph Wood Krutch. New York: Bantam Books, 1982. First published 1854.

Watson, Lyall. *Heaven's Breath: A Natural History of the Wind*. Introduction by Nick Hunt. New York: New York Review Books, 2019. First published 1984.

The Way of a Pilgrim. Translated by R. M. French. New York: HarperOne, 2010. First published 1954 by Harper.

First Snow

Beston, Henry. *The Best of Beston: A Selection from the Natural World of Henry Beston from Cape Cod to the St. Lawrence*. Edited and introduced by Elizabeth Coatsworth. Jaffrey, NH: Nonpareil Books, 2000.

Ishida, Tamotsu. "Acoustic Properties of Snow." Hokkaido University. March 30, 1965. https://tinyurl.com/2p8wmsvj.

Macfarlane, Robert. *The Wild Places*. London: Penguin Books, 2007.

May, Katherine. *Wintering: The Power of Rest and Retreat in Difficult Times*. London: Rider Books, 2020.

Maysenhölder, W., M. Schneebeli, X. Zhou, T. Zhang, and M. Heggli. "Sound Absorption of Snow." Fraunhofer-Institut für Bauphysik IBP. Accessed December 6, 2020. https://tinyurl.com/mr3hknap.

Thoreau, Henry David. *Walden and Other Writings*. Edited and with introduction by Joseph Wood Krutch. New York: Bantam Books, 1982. First published 1854.

———. *Winter: From the Journal of Henry David Thoreau*. Edited by Harrison G. O. Blake. Boston: Houghton Mifflin Company, 1887.

Dawn

Ackerman, Diane. "World at Dawn: The Pleasure of Life Rekindled." *Orion Magazine*, July/August 2009. https://tinyurl.com/mt6vuuhe.

Carmichael, Alexander. *Carmina Gadelica*. Vols. 1 and 2. Edinburgh, 1899.

Eckhart, Meister. *Meister Eckhart, from Whom God Hid Nothing: Sermons, Writings, and Sayings*. Foreword by David Steindl-Rast, OSB. Boston: New Seed Books, 1996.

Merton, Thomas. *A Book of Hours*. Edited by Kathleen Deignan, foreword by James Finley. Notre Dame, IN: Sorin Books, 2007.

———. *Conjectures of a Guilty Bystander*. Garden City, NY: Doubleday, 1966.

Newell, J. Philip. *Celtic Benediction: Morning and Night Prayer*. Grand Rapids, MI: William B. Eerdmans, 2000.

O'Donoghue, Noel Dermot. *The Mountain behind the Mountain: Aspects of the Celtic Tradition*. Edinburgh: T&T Clark, 1993.

Rilke, Rainer Maria. *Rilke's Book of Hours: Love Poems to God*. Translated by Anita Barrows and Joanna Macy. New York: Riverhead Books, 2005.

Steindl-Rast, David, and Sharon Lebell. *Music of Silence: A Sacred Journey through the Hours of the Day*. Introduction by Kathleen Norris. Berkeley, CA: Ulysses Press, 2002.

Underhill, Evelyn. *Worship*. Guildford, Surrey, UK: Eagle, 1991. First published 1936 by James Nisbet and Company.

Dusk

Deakin, Roger. *Wildwood: A Journey through Trees*. New York: Free Press, 2007.

Heschel, Abraham Joshua. *The Sabbath: Its Meaning for Modern Man*. Introduction by Susannah Heschel. New York: Farrar, Straus and Giroux, 2005. First published 1951.

Lunetta, Patricia. "The Visit." *Journey through Grief*. Accessed March 3, 2021. https://tinyurl.com/yc6wtd4a.

Steindl-Rast, David, and Sharon Lebell. *Music of Silence: A Sacred Journey through the Hours of the Day*. Introduction by Kathleen Norris. Berkeley, CA: Ulysses Press, 2002.

Whitman, Walt. *Specimen Days and Collect*. New York: Dover Publications, 1995. First published 1883 in Glasgow by Wilson & McCormick.

Wiederkehr, Macrina. *Seven Sacred Pauses: Living Mindfully through the Hours of the Day*. Notre Dame, IN: Sorin Books, 2008.

Zellman, Rabbi Reuben. "Holy Is Twilight." In *Mishkan Halev: Prayers for S'lichot and the Month of Elul*. New York: CCAR Press, 2017.

STARS

Beston, Henry. *The Best of Beston: A Selection from the Natural World of Henry Beston from Cape Cod to the St. Lawrence.* Edited and introduced by Elizabeth Coatsworth. Jaffrey, NH: Nonpareil Books, 2000.

Dillard, Annie. *Pilgrim at Tinker Creek.* New York: HarperCollins, 1998. First published 1974 by Harper's Magazine Press.

Hirsch, Edward. "In Spite of Everything, the Stars." In *Wild Gratitude.* New York: Alfred A. Knopf, 1986.

Koren, Marina. "How to Measure All the Starlight in the Universe." *Atlantic,* November 30, 2018. https://tinyurl.com/4w3m8k2a.

Lane, Belden C. *The Great Conversation: Nature and the Care of the Soul.* New York: Oxford University Press, 2019.

———. *Ravished by Beauty: The Surprising Legacy of Reformed Spirituality.* New York: Oxford University Press, 2011.

Rey, H. A. *The Stars: A New Way to See Them.* Boston: Houghton Mifflin, 1980. First published 1952.

Rogers, Pattiann. *Song of the World Becoming: New and Collected Poems; 1981–2001.* Minneapolis: Milkweed Editions, 2001.

MOON

Bahnson, Fred. "On the Road with Thomas Merton." *Emergence Magazine,* February 3, 2019. https://tinyurl.com/2hpbu49a.

Carmichael, Alexander. *Carmina Gadelica.* Vols 1 and 2. Edinburgh, 1899.

Macfarlane, Robert. *The Wild Places.* London: Penguin Books, 2007.

Merton, Thomas. *Woods, Shore, Desert: A Notebook, May 1968.* Santa Fe: Museum of New Mexico Press, 1982.

Mooney, James. *Myths of the Cherokee.* Washington, DC: Government Printing Office, 1902; Project Gutenberg, May 11, 2014. https://tinyurl.com/2p94j63v.

Newell, J. Philip. *The Book of Creation: An Introduction to Celtic Spirituality.* New York: Paulist Press, 1999.

Whitman, Walt. *Specimen Days and Collect*. New York: Dover Publications, 1995. First published 1883 in Glasgow by Wilson & McCormick.

LAMENTATIONS

Abram, David. *The Spell of the Sensuous: Perception and Language in a More-Than-Human World*. New York: Vintage Books, 2017. First published 1996.

―――. "The Ecology of Perception: An Interview with David Abram." By Emmanuel Vaughan-Lee. *Emergence Magazine*, July 20, 2020. https://tinyurl.com/yjc4d3ef.

American Bird Conservancy. "Glass Collisions: Preventing Bird Window Strikes." Accessed March 6, 2021. https://tinyurl.com/mt8ctd6y.

Berry, Thomas. *The Great Work: Our Way into the Future*. New York: Crown Publishing, 1999.

Beston, Henry. *The Best of Beston: A Selection from the Natural World of Henry Beston from Cape Cod to the St. Lawrence*. Edited and introduced by Elizabeth Coatsworth. Jaffrey, NH: Nonpareil Books, 2000.

Beswetherick, Michael, Matt McCann, Jesse Pesta, Nadja Popovich, and Rumsey Taylor. "California's Epic Wildfires in 2020 Took Deadly Aim at the State's Most Beloved Trees." *New York Times*, December 9, 2020. https://tinyurl.com/4fdpkun8.

Christie, Douglas E. *The Blue Sapphire of the Mind: Notes for a Contemplative Ecology*. New York: Oxford University Press, 2013.

Dickens, Charles. *Bleak House*. Hertfordshire, UK: Wordsworth, 1993. First published 1853 by Bradbury & Evans.

Dowd, Michelle. "The Thing with Feathers: On Mountains, Climate Science and Hope." *Alpinist*, November 27, 2019. https://tinyurl.com/mrrryv8h.

Hogan, Linda. *Dwellings: A Spiritual History of the Living World*. New York: W. W. Norton, 1995.

Kingsnorth, Paul. "The Myth of Progress: An Interview with Paul Kingsnorth." *Emergence Magazine*, August 22, 2018. https://tinyurl.com/yckpzcmn.

Ladinsky, Daniel, trans. *Love Poems from God: Twelve Sacred Voices from the East and West*. London: Penguin Compass, 2002.

Lane, Belden C. *The Great Conversation: Nature and the Care of the Soul.* New York: Oxford University Press, 2019.

Leopold, Aldo. *A Sand County Almanac.* New York: Oxford University Press, 1966. First published 1949.

Macfarlane, Robert. *The Wild Places.* London: Penguin Books, 2007.

Mahany, Barbara. "Chicago's Crowded Skies." *Chicago Tribune,* November 15, 2009. https://tinyurl.com/4bbcbb92.

Muir, John. *John of the Mountains: The Unpublished Journals of John Muir.* Madison: University of Wisconsin Press, 1966. First published 1938 by Houghton Mifflin.

National Oceanic and Atmospheric Administration. "Billion-dollar Weather and Climate Disasters: Overview." Accessed March 6, 2021. https://tinyurl.com/2p89kde6.

Teilhard de Chardin, Pierre. *The Divine Milieu.* New York: Harper & Row, 1960.

———. *The Human Phenomenon.* Translated by Sarah Appleton-Weber. Brighton, UK: Sussex Academic Press, 1999.

Thoreau, Henry David. *Walden and Other Writings.* Edited and with introduction by Joseph Wood Krutch. New York: Bantam Books, 1982. First published 1854.

Vaughan-Lee, Llewellyn. "A Ghost's Life." *Emergence Magazine,* December 17, 2020. https://tinyurl.com/yrpz6vuw.

A FEW WORDS OF GRATITUDE AND GRACE . . .

I cannot turn the last page on this book without profound and eternal thanks to Lauren Winner, my editor, whose brilliance is matched by her kindness, whose penetrating insights and understanding drew from me and from the text essential and imperative shaping. In a life list of editors—that genus without whom writers would flounder and fall to the earth—Lauren stands as one of the rarest. To Lil Copan, for saying yes, and reaching always toward the numinous. To all the wunderkinds behind the curtains at Broadleaf Books, especially Marissa Wold Uhrina, Travis Ables, James Kegley, and David Cottingham, as well as Kristin Goble of PerfecType, who made these pages beautiful and without errant commas, and nudged this book across the finish line. To Rabbi Rami Shapiro for planting the seed. To Mónica Russel y Rodríguez for an essential first read. To those guardian-angel first responders of literary ilk, especially Jan Sugar and Nancy Watkins, who untangle me from my self-inflicted writerly knots; and to Dr. Peter C. Nelson for checking my math and my physics. To my brother David Mahany, whose knowledge of Latin is a beautiful thing. And, with every grace, to Blair Kamin, my beloved, who kept me upright and fed, especially in the final days of a very long year, and who leapt in with his own editing excellence; for all that and for one other everything: for taking that long-ago leap, and wedding your life and your faith to the Irish Catholic who couldn't help but embrace all things Jewish. It was Judaism itself, that ancient and elemental wisdom tradition, that first unfurled for me the holiest text of the great Book of All God's Creation. I'll not lift my eyes from those pages that mesmerize and instruct without end. Always and ever, to Will and to Teddy, who are at the beating heart of all that I do and I am. To my blessed mama, the Original Mother Nature, who opened the book for me long before I knew its name. And, always, to the circle of soulmates who have pointed me to the richest titles on my bookshelves, and kept me in fine company, page after page.

All creation holds its breath, listening within me,
because, to hear you, I keep silent.

—Rainer Maria Rilke, twentieth-century
Austrian poet and novelist